My
iPad® 2

Gary Rosenzweig

que

800 East 96th Street,
Indianapolis, Indiana 46240 USA

My iPad 2®

Copyright © 2011 by Pearson Education, Inc.

ISBN-13: 978-0-7897-4116-5
ISBN-10: 0-7897-4116-4

Library of Congress Cataloging-in-Publication Data is on file and available upon request.

Printed in the United States of America

First Printing: April 2011

Trademarks

Warning and Disclaimer

Bulk Sales

Que Publishing offers excellent discounts on this book when ordered in quantity for bulk purchases or special sales. For more information, please contact

U.S. Corporate and Government Sales
1-800-382-3419
corpsales@pearsontechgroup.com

For sales outside of the U.S., please contact

International Sales
international@pearson.com

ASSOCIATE PUBLISHER
Greg Wiegand

ACQUISITIONS EDITOR
Laura Norman

MANAGING EDITOR
Kristy Hart

PROJECT EDITOR
Lori Lyons

PROOFREADER
Language Logistics, LLC

SENIOR INDEXER
Cheryl Lenser

PUBLISHING COORDINATOR
Cindy Teeters

BOOK DESIGNER
Anne Jones

COMPOSITOR
Nonie Ratcliff

Contents at a Glance

Chapter 1   Getting Started 3

Chapter 2   Customizing Your iPad 21

Chapter 3   Networking and Syncing 41

Chapter 4   Playing Music and Video 59

Chapter 5   Reading Books 81

Chapter 6   Organizing Your Life 97

Chapter 7   Surfing the Web 113

Chapter 8   Communicating with Email 135

Chapter 9   Taking and Viewing Photos 149

Chapter 10   Recording Video 167

Chapter 11   Writing with Pages 189

Chapter 12   Spreadsheets with Numbers 215

Chapter 13   Presentations with Keynote 243

Chapter 14   Navigating with Maps 263

Chapter 15   Getting, Organizing, and Using Apps 277

Chapter 16   Using Popular and Critical Apps 295

Chapter 17   Games and Entertainment Apps 333

Chapter 18   iPad Accessories 353

              Index 370

Table of Contents

1 Getting Started **3**

The iPad Buttons and Switches 4

The Home Button 4

The Wake/Sleep Button 5

The Volume Control 6

The Side Switch 6

Orientation and Movement 7

Screen Gestures 7

Tapping and Touching 8

Pinching 8

Dragging and Flicking 8

iPad Screens 9

The Lock Screen 9

The Home Screen 10

An App Screen 10

The Search Screen 11

The Settings Screen 12

Interacting with Your iPad 13

Common Interface Elements 13

Using the On Screen Keyboard 15

Editing Text 16

Copy and Paste 17

2 Customizing Your iPad **21**

Changing Your Wallpaper 22

Getting Details About Your iPad 24

Setting Alert Sounds 26

Password Protecting Your iPad 28

Setting Parental Restrictions 30

Setting Side Switch Functionality 32

Setting Your Date and Time 33

Modifying Keyboard Settings 34

Changing Safari Settings 36

Changing iPod Settings 37

More Settings 38

3 Networking and Syncing **41**

Setting Up Your Wi-Fi Network Connection 42

Setting Up Your 3G Connection 44

Syncing with iTunes 46

Syncing Contacts, Calendars, and Other Information . . 48

Syncing Apps 50

Syncing Documents 51

Syncing Music 52

Syncing Photos 53

Syncing Using MobileMe 55

4 Playing Music and Video **59**

Playing a Song 60

Building a Playlist 63

Making iTunes Purchases 65

Downloading Podcasts 69

Playing Video 72

Viewing YouTube Videos 74

Using AirPlay to Play Music and Video on
    Other Devices 76

Home Sharing 77

5 Reading Books **81**

Buying a Book from Apple 82

Reading a Book 85

Using Reading Aids 87

Adding Notes and Highlights 89

Adding Bookmarks 91

Organizing Your Books 92

Using iBooks Alternatives 94

6   Organizing Your Life **97**

Adding a Contact 98

Searching for a Contact 100

Working with Contacts 101

Creating a Calendar Event 102

Using Calendar Views 105

Day View 105

Week View 106

Month View 107

List View 108

Creating Notes 109

7   Surfing the Web **113**

Browsing to a URL 114

Searching the Web 115

Viewing Web Pages 117

Returning to Previously Visited Websites 120

Bookmarking Websites 122

Delete Your Bookmarks 123

Delete a Single Bookmark 123

Another Way to Delete Bookmarks 124

Creating Home Screen Bookmarks 125

Filling in Web Forms 126

Opening Multiple Web Pages 129

Copying Text and Images from Web Pages 131

Using Images from Web Pages 132

8   Communicating with Email **135**

Configuring Your Email 136

Reading Your Email 139

Composing a New Message 140

Creating a Signature 141

Deleting and Moving Messages 142

Searching Email 143

Configuring How Email Is Received 144

More Email Settings 145

9   Taking and Viewing Photos **149**

Taking Photos 149

Using Photo Booth 152

Browsing Your Photos 154

Using the Photos App 157

Viewing Albums 159

Creating a Slideshow 160

Turning Your iPad into a Picture Frame 161

Capturing the Screen 163

Deleting Photos 164

10   Recording Video **167**

Shooting Video 168

Trimming Video Clips 170

Combining Clips in iMovie 171

Editing Transitions in iMovie 175

Adding Photos to Your Video in iMovie 177

Adding Video Titles in iMovie 180

Creating a FaceTime Account 181

Placing Video Calls with FaceTime 183

Receiving Video Calls with FaceTime 185

11   Writing with Pages **189**

Creating a New Document 190

Styling Text 192

Reusing Styles 195

Formatting Text 196

Creating Lists 198

Column Layouts 200

Inserting Images 201

Using Shapes in Documents 204

Creating Tables 205

Creating Charts 207

Document Setup 209

Transferring Documents to Pages with iTunes 210

Transferring Documents from Pages to iTunes 212

12   Spreadsheets with Numbers **215**

Creating a New Spreadsheet 216

Totaling Columns 220

Averaging Columns 221

Performing Calculations 225

Formatting Tables 226

    Formatting Cells 226

    Formatting Whole Tables 229

    Using Headers and Footers 230

Creating Forms 231

Creating Charts 234

Using Multiple Tables 236

13   Presentations with Keynote **243**

Building a Simple Presentation 244

Building Your Own Slide 246

Adding Transitions 250

    Magic Move 251

    Object Transitions 253

Organizing Slides 255

Playing Your Presentation 257

Presenting on an External Display 258

14   Navigating with Maps **263**

Finding a Location 264

Searching for Places and Things 266

Getting Directions 267

Setting Bookmarks 269

Using Views 271

   Using Satellite View 271

   Using Street View 273

Getting Traffic Reports 275

15 The World of Apps **277**

Purchasing an App 278

Arranging Apps on Your iPad 281

Arranging Apps Using iTunes 282

Creating App Folders 284

Viewing Currently Running Apps 285

Finding Good Apps 286

Using iPhone/iPod touch Apps 288

Getting Help with Apps 290

Telling Friends About Apps 291

16 Using Popular and Critical Apps **295**

Using iTap VNC 296

Using Bento 298

Using GoodReader 301

Using NewsRack 303

Using Flipboard 307

Using OmniGraffle 309

Adding a Dictionary and Thesaurus 311

Using MindNode 313

Using Skype 315

Putting Notes on Your Home/Lock Screen 317

Talking to Your iPad 321

Recording Voice Memos 323

Handwriting Notes 325

Using Epicurious 327

Other Useful Apps 329

17   Games and Entertainment **333**

Composing Music with GarageBand 334

Watching Movies and TV Shows with Netflix 337

Reading Comics 339

Listening to Music with Pandora Radio 340

Using Game Center 342

Playing iPad Games 344

Air Hockey 344

Highborn 345

Harbor Master 346

Angry Birds 346

Galcon Fusion 347

Plants vs. Zombies 348

Monkey Island 2 Special Edition 348

Scrabble 349

Field Runners 349

Real Racing 2 HD 350

Gold Strike 350

18   iPad Accessories **353**

Printing from Your iPad 354

iPad Smart Cover 357

Apple iPad 2 Dock 358

Apple Video Output Adapters 359

Dock to VGA Adapter 359

Digital AV Adapters 360

Apple Wireless Keyboard 361

Apple iPad Keyboard Dock 364

Power/Dock Accessories 365

Protecting Your iPad 366

Apple iPad Camera Connection Kit 368

Index **370**

About the Author

Gary Rosenzweig is an Internet entrepreneur, software developer, and technology writer. He runs CleverMedia, Inc., which produces websites, computer games, and podcasts.

CleverMedia's largest site, MacMost.com, features video tutorials for Apple enthusiasts. It includes many videos on using Macs, iPhones, and iPads.

Gary has written numerous computer books, including *ActionScript 3.0 Game Programming University*, *MacMost.com Guide to Switching to the Mac*, and *Special Edition Using Director MX*.

Gary lives in Denver, Colorado, with his wife, Debby, and daughter, Luna. He has a computer science degree from Drexel University and a master's degree in journalism from the University of North Carolina at Chapel Hill.

Website: http://garyrosenzweig.com

Twitter: http://twitter.com/rosenz

More iPad Tutorials and Book Updates: http://macmost.com/ipadguide/

Dedication

To Randy Cassingham and the members of "The Cabal Of Which We Do Not Speak."
Whether you run your own business, or just work on projects in your spare time, it is
important to have a peer group of top-notch, smart, and generous individuals. I am so
grateful that I have mine.

Acknowledgments

Thanks, as always, to my wife, Debby, and my daughter, Luna. Also thanks to the rest of my family: Jacqueline Rosenzweig, Jerry Rosenzweig, Larry Rosenzweig, Tara Rosenzweig, Rebecca Jacob, Barbara Shifrin, Richard Shifrin, Barbara H. Shifrin, Tage Thomsen, Anne Thomsen, Andrea Thomsen, and Sami Balestri.

Thanks to all the people who watch the show and participate at the MacMost website. Special thanks to Valerie Lapcevich, Jim Lanford, Anne Mitchell, and all of my Twitter friends who helped during the writing of this book. Thanks to the Cherry Creek Apple Store in Denver, Colorado.

Thanks to everyone at Pearson Education who worked on this book: Laura Norman, Lori Lyons, Chrissy Andry, Nonie Ratcliff, Kristy Hart, Matthew David, Cindy Teeters, Anne Jones, and Greg Wiegand.

We Want to Hear from You!

As the reader of this book, *you* are our most important critic and commentator. We value your opinion and want to know what we're doing right, what we could do better, what areas you'd like to see us publish in, and any other words of wisdom you're willing to pass our way.

As an associate publisher for Que Publishing, I welcome your comments. You can email or write me directly to let me know what you did or didn't like about this book—as well as what we can do to make our books better.

Please note that I cannot help you with technical problems related to the topic of this book. We do have a User Services group, however, where I will forward specific technical questions related to the book.

When you write, please be sure to include this book's title and author as well as your name, email address, and phone number. I will carefully review your comments and share them with the author and editors who worked on the book.

Email: feedback@quepublishing.com

Mail: Greg Wiegand
            Associate Publisher
            Que Publishing
            800 East 96th Street
            Indianapolis, IN 46240 USA

Reader Services

Visit our website and register this book at quepublishing.com/register for convenient access to any updates, downloads, or errata that might be available for this book.

Learn to tap, swipe,
flick, and pinch
your way through
the iPad's interface.

Learn to use the iPad's
physical switches.

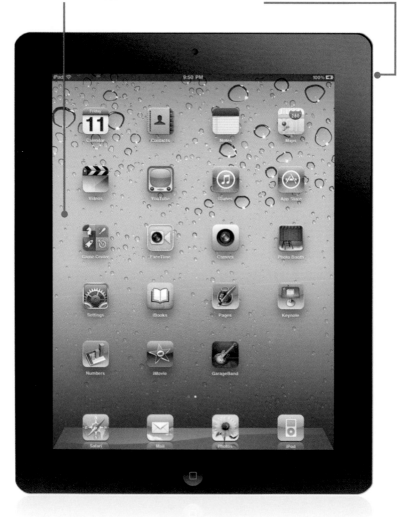

In this chapter you learn how to perform specific tasks on your iPad to become familiar with the interface.

→ The iPad Buttons and Switches

→ Screen Gestures

→ iPad Screens

→ Interacting with Your iPad

Getting Started

Before you learn how to perform specific tasks on your iPad, you should become familiar with the interface. If you have used an iPhone or iPod Touch, you already know the basics. But if the iPad is your first touch-screen device, you need to take time to become accustomed to interacting with it.

The iPad Buttons and Switches

The iPad features a Home button, a Wake/Sleep button, a volume control, and side switch.

Wake/Sleep

Side Switch

Volume control

Home button

The Home Button

The Home button is probably the most important physical control on the iPad and the one that you will use the most often. Pressing the Home button returns you to the Home screen of the iPad when you are inside an application, such as Safari or Mail, and you want to get back to your Home screen to launch another app. You can also double press the Home button to see icons for your other applications and controls for audio or video playback, without leaving the current application.

Where's the Quit Button?

Few, if any, apps on the iPad have a way to quit. Instead, think of the Home button as the Quit button. It closes out the current app and returns you to your Home screen. The app is actually still running, but paused, in the background. To completely quit an app, see "Viewing Currently Running Apps," in Chapter 15.

The Wake/Sleep Button

The primary function of the Wake/Sleep button (sometimes called the On/Off button) at the top of your iPad is to quickly put it to sleep. Sleeping is different than shutting down. When your iPad is in sleep mode, you can instantly wake it to use it. You can wake up from sleep by pressing the Wake/Sleep button again or pressing the Home button.

The Wake/Sleep button can also be used to shut down your iPad, which you might want to do if you leave your iPad for a long time and want to preserve the battery life.

Press and hold the Wake/Sleep button for a few seconds, and the iPad begins to shut down and turn off. Confirm your decision to shut down your iPad using the Slide to Power Off button on the screen.

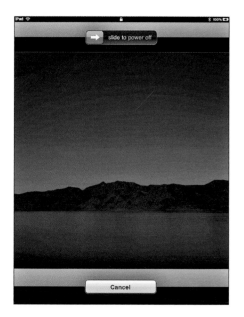

To start up your iPad, press and hold the Wake/Sleep button for a few seconds until you see something appear on the screen.

When Should I Turn Off My iPad?

It is perfectly normal to never turn off your iPad. While in sleep mode, with the screen off, it uses little power. If you can plug it in to power at night or during longer periods when you are not carrying it with you, you don't need to ever shut it down.

The Volume Control

The volume control on the side of your iPad is actually two buttons: one to turn the volume up, and the other to turn it down.

Your iPad keeps two separate volume settings in memory: one for head-phones and one for the internal speakers. If you turn down the volume when using headphones and then unplug the headphones, the volume changes to reflect the last settings used when headphones were not plugged in and vice versa. A Speaker icon and a series of rectangles display on the screen to indi-cate the level of volume.

The Side Switch

The switch on the side of your iPad can do one of two things: It can be set as a mute switch or an orientation lock. You can decide which function this but-ton performs in your iPad's settings. See "Setting Side Switch Functionality" in Chapter 2.

If you choose to use this switch as a mute switch, it will mute all sound if switched to the off position. You will see a speaker icon appear briefly in the middle of the screen when you do this. A line through the icon means you just muted the sound; otherwise, you just unmuted your iPad. By default, the iPad 2 comes with the switch configured to mute.

If you choose to use this switch as an orientation lock, it will do something else entirely. Your iPad has two primary screen modes: vertical and horizontal. You can use almost every default app in either orientation. For example, if you find that a web page is too wide to fit on the screen in vertical orientation, you can turn the iPad sideways and the view changes to a horizontal orientation.

When you don't want your iPad to react to its orientation, slide the iPad side switch so that you can see the orange dot, which prevents the orientation from changing. When you need to unlock it, just slide the lock off.

This comes in handy in many situations. For instance, if you are reading an ebook in bed or on a sofa while lying on your side, then you may want vertical orientation even though the iPad is lying sideways.

Orientation and Movement

I know I said there were only four physical switches on your iPad, but there is another one: the entire iPad.

Your iPad knows which way it is oriented, and it knows if it is being moved. The simplest indication of this is that it knows whether you hold it vertically with the Home button at the bottom or horizontally with the Home button to one of the sides. Some apps, especially games, use the exact screen orientation of the iPad to guide screen elements and views.

Shake It Up!

One interesting physical gesture you might perform is the "shake." Because your iPad can sense movement, it can sense when you shake it. Many apps take advantage of this feature and use it to set off an action, such as shuffling songs in the iPod app or erasing a drawing canvas.

Screen Gestures

Who knew just a few years ago that we'd be controlling computing devices with taps, pinches, and flicks rather than drags, key presses, and clicks? Multitouch devices such as the iPhone, iPod Touch, and the iPad have added a new vocabulary to human-computer interaction.

Tapping and Touching

Since there is no mouse, a touch screen has no cursor. When your finger is not on the screen, there is no arrow pointing to anything.

A single, quick touch on the screen is usually called a "tap" or a "touch." You usually tap an object on the screen to perform an action.

Occasionally you need to double-tap—two quick taps in the same location. For instance, double-tapping an image on a web page zooms in to the image. Another double-tap zooms back out.

Pinching

The screen on the iPad is a multitouch screen, which means it can detect more than one touch at the same time. This capability is used all the time with the pinch gesture.

A pinch (or a pinch in) is when you touch the screen with both your thumb and index finger and move them toward each other in a pinching motion. You can also pinch in reverse, which is sometimes called an "unpinch" or "pinch out."

An example of when you would use a pinch would be to zoom in and out on a web page or photograph.

Dragging and Flicking

If you touch the screen and hold your finger down, you can drag it in any direction along the screen. This action often has the effect of moving the content on the screen.

For instance, if you are viewing a long web page and drag up or down, the page will scroll. Sometimes an app will let you drag content left and right as well.

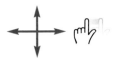

What if you have a long web page or a list of items inside an app? Instead of dragging the length of the screen, lifting your finger up, and moving it to the bottom to drag again, you can "flick." Flicking is like dragging, but you move quickly and lift your finger off the screen at the last moment so that the content continues to scroll after you have lifted your finger. You can wait for it to stop scrolling or touch the screen to make it stop.

iPad Screens

Unlike a computer, the iPad screen does only one thing at a time. Let's go through some of the typical screens you see while getting to know your iPad.

The Lock Screen

The default state of your iPad when you are not using it is the lock screen. This is just a picture with the time at the top and a large slider at the bottom with the words "slide to unlock" and single button to the right of the slider for launching a picture frame photo slideshow (see Chapter 9, "Taking and Viewing Photos").

By default you see the lock screen when you wake up your iPad. Sliding the unlock slider takes you to the Home screen or to whichever app you were using when you put the iPad to sleep.

The Home Screen

Think of the Home screen as a single screen but with multiple pages that each features different app icons. At the bottom of the Home screen are app icons that do not change from page to page. The area resembles the Mac OS X Dock.

The number of pages on your Home screen depends on how many apps you have. The number of pages you have is indicated by the white dots near the bottom of the screen, just above the bottom icons. The brightest dot represents the page you are currently viewing. You can move between pages on your Home screen by dragging or flicking left or right.

To the left of the dots is a small magnifying glass that represents the search screen. We talk about that in a minute.

An App Screen

When you tap on an app icon on the Home screen, you run that app just like you would run an application on your computer. The app takes over the entire screen.

At this point your screen can look like anything. If you run Safari, for instance, a web page displays. If you run Mail, you see a list of your new email or a single incoming email message.

The Search Screen

If you are on your Home screen, looking at page one of your app icons, you can drag to the right to get to the Search screen, which has a Search iPad field at the top and a keyboard at the bottom.

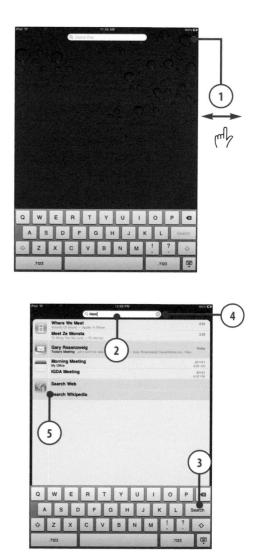

You can type in anything to search for a contact, app, email message, photo, and so on. You don't have to define what type of thing you want to search for.

1. From the Home screen, drag left to right to go to the Search screen.

2. Type a search term using the on-screen keyboard.

3. You see a list of items on your iPad that match the search term. Tap the Search button on the key-board to dismiss the keyboard and complete the search.

4. Tap the X in the search field to clear the search and start again.

5. Tap any of the items to go to the appropriate app and view the content.

The Settings Screen

One of the apps that you have on your iPad by default is the Settings app. With the Settings app, you can control several basic preferences for your iPad. (See Chapter 2, "Customizing Your iPad," for more on customizing settings.)

This is really just another app screen, but it is worth singling out as you'll need it to customize most aspects of your iPad.

Interacting with Your iPad

Now let's examine the different types of on-screen interface elements, the on-screen keyboard and how to use it, and specialized interactions such as text editing and copy and paste.

Common Interface Elements

Several interface elements are more complex than a simple button. In typical Apple style, these elements are often self-explanatory, but if you have never used an iPhone or iPod touch before, you might find some that give you pause.

Sliders

A slider is really just a button. But instead of tapping it, you need to tap and drag to the right to indicate that you want to perform the action, which makes it harder to accidentally trigger the action.

The most obvious example is the slider at the bottom of the Lock screen. If there were a button there, it might be too easy to unlock your iPad without realizing it.

Switches

A switch is also like a simple button, but you need to tap only the switch to activate it. A switch gives you feedback about which state it is in.

For example, switches indicate whether the Sound Check and Lyrics & Podcast Info features of the iPod are on or off. Tapping on either switch changes the position of the switch.

Sound Check	OFF
EQ	Off >
Volume Limit	Off >
Lyrics & Podcast Info	ON

Toolbars

Some apps have a set of buttons in a toolbar at the top of the screen that are general controls. The toolbar might disappear or the buttons might vary depending on the mode of the app. An example of a toolbar is in the iTunes app.

Menus

Often tapping a single button in a toolbar brings up more buttons or a list of choices, which are like menus on your Mac or PC. The choices in the list are usually related. For example, a button in Safari gives you options to Add Bookmark, Add to Home Screen, or Mail Link to This Page.

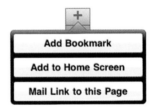

Tab Bars

Sometimes you see a row of buttons at the bottom of the screen that function similarly to toolbars, but each button represents a different mode for the app. For instance, at the bottom of the YouTube app, you see a Tab bar that you use to switch between various lists of videos: Featured, Top Rated, Most Viewed, Favorites, Subscriptions, My Videos, and History.

Using the On Screen Keyboard

The interface element you might interact with the most is the on-screen keyboard. It pops up from the bottom of the screen automatically whenever you need to enter some text.

The default keyboard has only letters and the most basic punctuation available. There are two shift keys that enable you to enter uppercase letters. You also have a Backspace key and a Return key.

Is There a Quicker Way to Capitalize?

So to capitalize a word, you tap the Shift key and then type the letter, right? You can. But a faster way is to tap the Shift key; then, without letting your finger off the screen, drag it to the letter and release in a single tap, slide, release action.

You can do the same with numbers and punctuation by tapping the .?123 key and sliding and releasing over the key you want.

To enter numbers and some other punctuation, tap the .?123 key to switch your keyboard into a second mode for numbers and punctuation.

To return to the letters, just tap the ABC key, or tap the #+= key to go to a third keyboard that includes less frequently used punctuation and symbols.

There are other keyboard variations. For instance, if you type in a location that needs a web address, a keyboard that doesn't have a spacebar appears that instead has commonly used symbols such as colons, slashes, underscores, and even a .com button. Instead of a Return key, you might see an action word like "Search" written on that key—tapping it will perform an action like searching the Web. All keyboards include a button at the bottom right that enables you to hide the keyboard if you want to dismiss it.

Editing Text

Editing text has its challenges on a touch-screen device. Even though you can just touch any portion of your text on screen, your finger tip is too large for the level of precision you usually get with a computer mouse and cursor. To compensate, Apple developed an editing technique using a magnifying glass area of the screen that you get when you touch and hold over a piece of text.

For example, if you want to enter some text into a field in Safari, touch and hold on the field. A circle of magnification appears with a cursor placed at the exact location you selected.

When you find the exact location that you want to indicate, release your finger from the screen. Then a variety of options display, depending on what
kind of text you selected, such as Select, Select All, and Paste. You can ignore
the options presented and start typing again to insert text at this location.

Copy and Paste

You can copy and paste text inside
an app, and between apps, on your
iPad. Here's how you might copy a
piece of text from one document to
another in the Notes app.

1. Launch Notes. If you don't have
   any notes yet, create one by typing some sample text.

2. Touch and hold over a word in
   your note. The Select/Select All
   pop-up menu appears.

3. Choose Select.

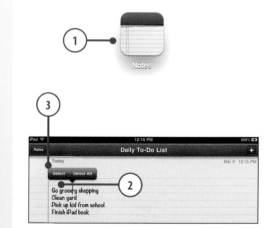

4. Some text appears highlighted surrounded by dots connected to lines. Tap and drag the dots so the highlighted area is exactly what you want.

5. Tap Copy.

6. Tap the + button to create a new note.

7. Tap the empty document area once to bring up a pop-up menu with the Paste command.

8. Tap Paste to insert the copied text.

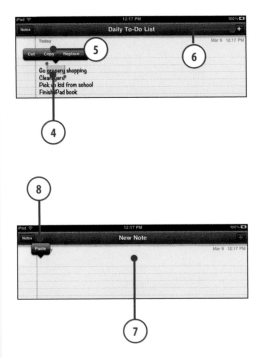

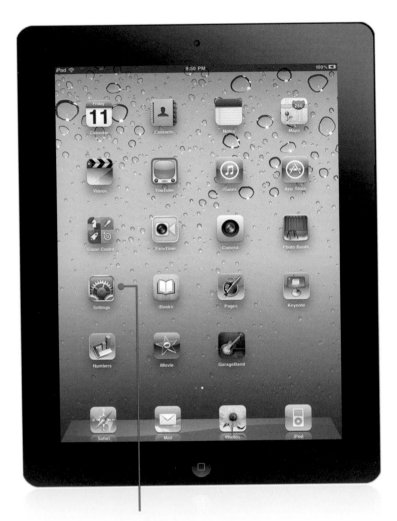

Customize how your iPad looks and works
through the Settings app.

In this chapter you learn how to change some of the settings on your iPad such as your background images, sounds, password, and how some apps behave.

2

→ Changing Your Wallpaper

→ Getting Details About Your iPad

→ Setting Alert Sounds

→ Password Protecting Your iPad

→ Setting Parental Restrictions

→ Setting Side Switch Functionality

→ Setting Your Date and Time

→ Modifying Keyboard Settings

→ Web Surfing Settings

→ Changing iPod Settings

Customizing Your iPad

Like with any relationship, you fall in love with your iPad for what it is. And then, almost immediately, you try to change it.

It's easier, though, to customize your iPad than it is your significant other because you can modify various settings and controls in the Settings app. You can also move icons around on the Home screen and even change how the Home button works.

Changing Your Wallpaper

The wallpaper is the image behind the icons on the Home screen and on the lock screen, so make sure it's something you like.

1. Tap the Settings icon on your Home screen.

2. Choose Brightness & Wallpaper from the Settings on the left side of the screen.

3. Tap the Large Wallpaper button that shows previews of your lock and home screens.

4. If you haven't yet loaded any pictures on to your iPad, you'll be taken right to step 5. Otherwise, to choose an Apple-supplied wallpaper, tap Wallpaper or choose a photo album and skip ahead to step 11.

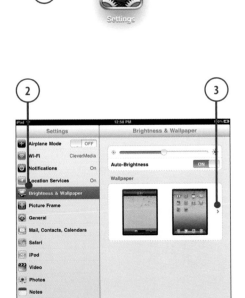

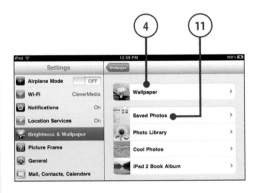

5. Tap an image icon to select it. You see a full view of the image.

6. From this full view, choose Set Lock Screen to set this image as the background of your lock screen.

7. Choose Set Home Screen to set this image as the background for your Home screen.

8. Choose Set Both to make the image the background for both screens.

9. Tap Cancel at the upper-left corner of the screen to go back to the wallpaper icons.

10. When viewing the list of icons, tap the Back button at the top of the screen to go back to the previous screen.

11. Tap Photo Library or a photo album to view your photos.

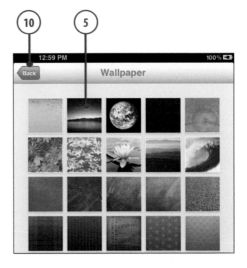

12. Tap a photo icon to view that photo from your photo album.

13. Use the buttons described in steps 6, 7, and 8 to set this image as a background.

Adjusting the Wallpaper Image

You can touch and drag in a photo to move to other areas of the image so you can choose the part of the image you want as your wallpaper. You can also pinch to zoom in and out on your photographs.

Getting Details About Your iPad

One of the many things in the Settings app on the iPad is an About section, from which you can learn details about your iPad.

1. Tap the Settings app on your Home screen.

2. Tap General from the list of settings on the left.

3. Tap About, the first button at the top of the list of General settings.

4. See how many songs, videos, photos, and apps you have.

5. See the total capacity of your iPad and the amount of space available.

Why Am I Missing Space?

Notice in the example here that the capacity of the iPad is shown as 14.0GB. However, that particular model is advertised as a "16GB" model. The discrepancy between the two is because of space used by the operating system and other system files.

iPad 2	
Songs	0
Videos	2
Photos	42
Applications	6
Capacity	14.0 GB
Available	12.8 GB
Version	4.3 (8F191)
Model	MC769LL
Serial Number	DLXFC25LDFHW
Wi-Fi Address	A4:67:06:05:5D:F2
Bluetooth	A4:67:06:05:5D:F3
Legal	>
Regulatory	>

6. The version number tells you which version of the iPad operating system you are running. Check this to make sure you are running the latest version of the iPad OS.

7. The model number tells you exactly which iPad you own if you happen to get it serviced or perhaps to report a bug to a third-party app developer.

8. The serial number, Wi-Fi address, and Bluetooth address are unique to your iPad. Apple may ask for your serial number if you are sending your iPad in for repairs. The Wi-Fi number is what you need if you are asked for a "MAC address" or "Ethernet address" for your iPad.

Another Model Number?

If you tap the Regulatory button on the About screen, you are taken to another screen that lists another model number for your iPad. For the iPad 2, Wi-Fi only model, this is A1395. The models A1396 and A1397 represent the AT&T and Verizon 3G models. When you are buying third-party accessories for your iPad, the specifications for those accessories may say "compatible with model X." In that case, X may represent either model number.

Setting Alert Sounds

Your iPad can be a noisy device with various events that trigger alert sounds. Just typing on the on-screen keyboard can produce a series of clicks.

Here's how to adjust your iPad's alert sounds.

1. Tap the Settings icon on the Home screen.

2. Tap General from the list of settings on the left.

3. Tap Sounds.

4. The volume slider is a separate control for incoming call rings from FaceTime.

5. When Change with Buttons is turned off, the ringer volume (see step 4) and alert volume (side volume buttons) are separate. When you turn this on, they are locked to the same setting, and you can use the slider to adjust both.

6. Tap Ringtone to see a list of ringtones that can be used when you have an incoming FaceTime call. For more information on FaceTime, see "Placing Video Calls with FaceTime," in Chapter 10.

7. Switch New Mail alert on or off to control if a sound plays when new mail arrives in the Mail app.

8. Switch Sent Mail sound on or off.

9. Switch Calendar Alerts on to allow audible alerts for calendar reminders to play. You can specify whether a specific event sounds an alert when you create that event in the Calendar app.

10. Switch the Lock Sounds on or off. When this setting is on, a sound plays when you unlock the Lock screen.

11. Switch Keyboard Clicks on or off.

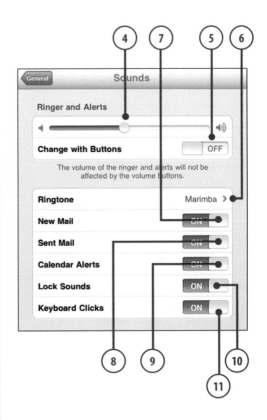

What? No Custom Sounds?

The current version of the iPad OS doesn't enable you to set custom sounds for any alerts. Hopefully at some point we can change these sounds or even have them reflect different properties of mail messages and calendar events.

Password Protecting Your iPad

Password protecting your iPad is a great way to make sure that someone else can't access your information or use your iPad.

1. Tap the Settings icon on the Home screen.

2. Tap General from the list of settings on the left.

3. Tap Passcode Lock.

Even More Security

To lock your iPad automatically when you aren't using it, choose Auto-Lock from the General Settings and set your iPad to automatically lock at 2, 5, 10, or 15 minutes. You can also choose to never have it auto-lock. Of course, you can manually lock your iPad at any time by pressing the Wake/Sleep button at the top.

4. Tap Simple Passcode to switch from using a 4-digit number to a longer password that can include both letters and numbers, if you want additional security; otherwise, your password will consist of 4 digits. Tap Turn Passcode On.

5. Type in a four-digit passcode that you can easily remember. Write it down and store it in a safe place as you can run into a lot of trouble if you forget it.

6. You will be asked to re-enter your passcode.

7. Tap the Require Passcode button and choose the delay before a passcode is required. If you choose anything other than Immediately, then someone else using your iPad can work on it for that period of time before needing to enter the code.

8. Turn off Picture Frame to remove the Picture Frame slideshow button on the Lock screen.

9. Turn on Erase Data if you want to erase the iPad data after 10 failed passcode attempts.

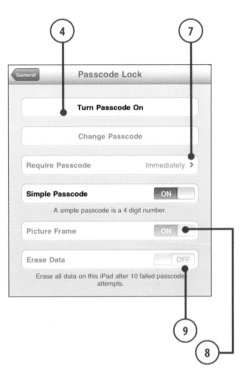

10. Press the Wake/Sleep button to confirm your new settings work. Then press the Home button and Slide to Unlock. The Enter Passcode screen displays.

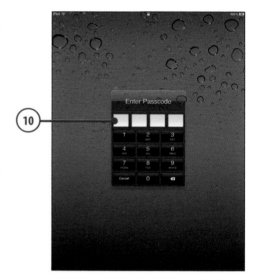

You Forgot Your Passcode?

Well, it wouldn't be secure if there were a way to get around the passcode, so you're out of luck until you can connect your iPad to your Mac or PC and use iTunes to restore it. Hopefully, this never happens to you.

Setting Parental Restrictions

If you plan to let your kids play with your iPad, you might want to set some restrictions on what they can do.

1. Tap the Settings icon on the Home screen.

2. Tap General.

3. Tap Restrictions.

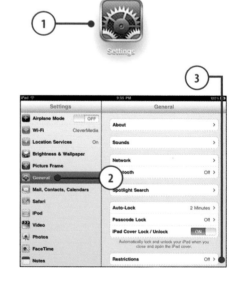

4. Tap Enable Restrictions to turn restrictions on or tap Disable Restrictions to turn them off.

5. Type in a four-digit code and then re-enter the code when prompted. Remember this code, or you can't turn off restrictions.

6. To remove the Safari, YouTube, Camera, FaceTime, and iTunes apps from your Home screen, turn the switches to off.

7. The Installing Apps switch prevents new apps from being installed.

8. The Location switch turns off location-based functions of all apps.

9. You can disallow adding or changing email accounts.

10. Use Allowed Content to determine whether In-App Purchases of paid app content, such as game levels or magazine issues, are allowed.

11. Pick which country's rating system to use from the Ratings For submenu.

12. On the last four items, choose the highest level of rating that a piece of content can have for it to be used. For instance, under Movies you can choose to allow only PG-13 or lower. You can also choose Allow All Movies or Don't Allow Movies.

13. Select options in the Game Center functions you want to allow. This will only affect games that use Game Center to communicate with other players. Some apps use their own system of communication or other systems like Facebook.

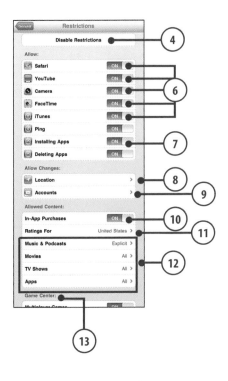

It's Not All Good

SETTINGS NOT REMEMBERED

It would be nice if you could just switch Restrictions on and off, so you could hand off your iPad to Junior after quickly turning them on, but the settings are reset each time. So you need to set the switches each time after turning Restrictions back on.

Setting Side Switch Functionality

When the original iPad came out, the side switch was an orientation lock. It was very useful for fixing the orientation while reading a book. But then Apple changed the functionality of the switch with a software update and turned it into a mute switch like the iPhone has. That made a lot of people unhappy. So with iOS 4.3 you get to choose what you want the side button to do.

1. Tap the Settings icon on the Home screen.

2. Tap General.

3. Choose Lock Rotation if you want your side switch to be an orientation lock switch.

4. Choose Mute if you want the side switch to mute the volume on the speakers and earphones.

Setting Your Date and Time

You can set the date, time and time zone for your iPad and even choose whether to display the time in 12- or 24-hour mode.

1. Tap the Settings icon on the Home screen.

2. Tap General.

3. Tap Date & Time.

4. Set the 24-Hour Time switch to your preference.

5. Tap the Time Zone button and then enter the name of your city, or a nearby city, to set the zone.

6. Tap the Set Date & Time to bring up date and time controls.

7. Tap either the day or the time at the top of the control to switch the bottom of the control to the correct interface. If you choose the time, you can set the hour and minute. If you choose the date, you can set the month, day, and year.

| 24-Hour Time | OFF |

| Time Zone | Denver > |

| Set Date & Time | > |

Date & Time

Friday, March 11, 2011

5:00 PM

⑦

3	58	
4	59	AM
5	00	PM
6	01	
7	02	

Set Automatically?

You may see Set Automatically on this screen instead of the Time Zone and Set Date & Time options. This would happen if you have a 3G model of the iPad 2 and have turned on your 3G service. You can leave it on to set the time automatically using your provider's time, or turn it off to reveal the manual time controls.

Modifying Keyboard Settings

If you use your iPad for email or word processing, you will use the on-screen keyboard a lot. The keyboard does several things to make it easier for you to type, but some of these might get in the way of your typing style. Use the following steps to modify the keyboard settings to your preferences.

1. Tap the Settings icon on the Home screen.

①

2. Tap General.

3. Tap Keyboard.

4. Turn Auto-Capitalization on to automatically make the first character of a name or a sentence a capital letter.

5. Turn Auto-Correction on to have mistyped words automatically corrected.

6. Turn on or off to control whether possible misspellings are indicated.

7. Turn Enable Caps Lock on or off. By default this is off. When Caps Lock is enabled, you double-tap the shift key to lock it.

8. Turn on the "." Shortcut if you want a double-tap of the spacebar to insert a period followed by a space.

9. Use the International Keyboards button to choose a different keyboard layout. In addition to keyboards commonly used in other countries, you can switch to a Dvorak keyboard or one of several other alternatives to the traditional QWERTY keyboard.

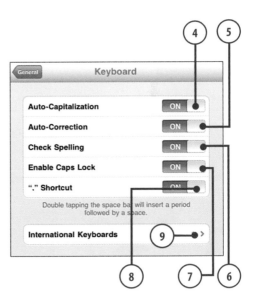

Changing Safari Settings

We look at the Safari Web browser in Chapter 7, "Surfing the Web," but you can customize it right here in the Settings app.

1. Tap the Settings icon on the Home screen.

2. Tap Safari from the list of settings on the left.

3. Select which search engine to use. Google is the default, but you can also choose Yahoo! or Bing.

4. Adjust your AutoFill settings for filling out forms on the Web. Your iPad can pull from your contact info in the Contacts app or from data you previously filled in on the same or similar Web pages. Set Names and Passwords to true to have Safari remember your username and passwords for some websites.

5. Choose whether to show the Bookmarks bar all the time or only when you have saved bookmarks in the bookmarks bar.

6. Fraud Warning checks websites against a public database of websites to avoid. I recommend leaving this switch on. If you try to follow a link to one of these sites, you get a warning and a chance to change your mind before loading the page.

Changing iPod Settings

You have a few preferences to choose from when it comes to iPod music playback. Most of them have to do with the quality and volume of sound you get from your iPad.

1. Tap the Settings icon on the Home screen.

2. Choose iPod from the list of settings on the left.

3. Turn Sound Check on or off to play your music at approximately the same volume level, even if the song files themselves are louder or softer than each other.

4. Use EQ to select an equalizer setting. You can select from an equalizer setting according to the type of music you listen to, or settings like "Spoken Word," "Small Speakers," or "Bass Booster."

5. Tap Volume Limit to set a limit on the maximum volume.

6. To set a Volume Limit, simply move the slider.

7. Tap the Lock Volume Limit to set a code required to change or remove the Volume Limit.

8. Enter a four-digit code and confirm.

9. Switch Lyrics & Podcast Info on or off. When this is on, you can tap the album artwork while a song or podcast is playing in the iPod app to see the information stored in the file, such as podcast summaries and information, song information, or lyrics.

10. Enter your Apple ID and password information to allow streaming music and video from your Mac. See "Home Sharing" in Chapter 4.

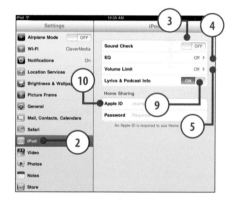

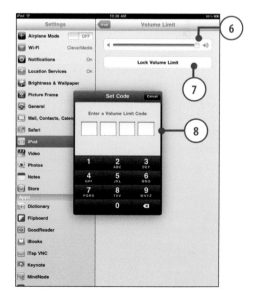

More Settings

Too many settings categories exist to cover all of them here, but the following are a few other key items.

1. Tap Video.

2. Adjust whether a video starts playing where you left off or at the beginning each time.

3. Turn Closed Captioning on or off.

4. Tap Photos.

5. Set the slideshow preferences: how long to play each slide for, whether to repeat, and in which order to play the photos.

Adding More and More Apps

The Settings app adds new pages as you add new apps to your iPad. Some third-party apps do not add a component in the Settings app, so don't be alarmed if you don't see an app you added in the Settings list.

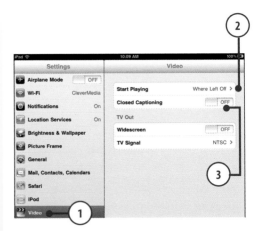

Sync your music and information
with your Mac or PC computer.

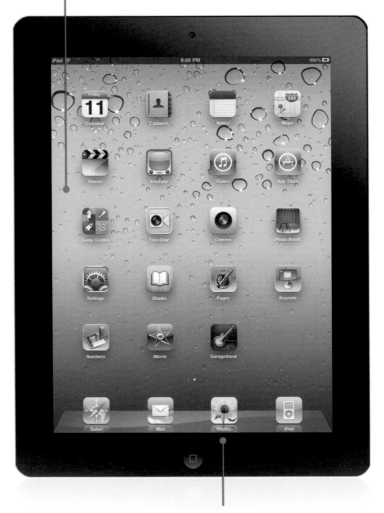

Put your favorite photos
on your iPad.

In this chapter you find out how to connect your iPad to your local Wi-Fi network. You also see how to sync your iPad with your Mac or Windows computer.

→ Setting Up Your Network Connection
→ Setting Up Your 3G Connection
→ Syncing with iTunes

Networking and Syncing

Now that you have a new iPad, why not introduce it to your old friend—your computer? They have a lot in common. And they are both good at sharing—particularly information such as your contacts, calendar, music, video, and documents.

Syncing your iPad to your Mac or PC is something you want to do right away and continue to do on a regular basis. This way you get all your data from your computer onto your iPad, and as you add new information and media to either device, they can share it so it is always at your fingertips.

Setting Up Your Wi-Fi Network Connection

One of the first things you need to do with your iPad, even before you sync it to your computer, is to establish an Internet connection.

All iPads have the ability to connect to the Internet through a Wi-Fi network, like the one you may already be using to connect your computers or iPhone.

To connect your iPad to your wireless network, follow these steps.

1. Tap the Settings icon on the Home screen.

2. Choose Wi-Fi from the list of settings on the left.

3. Make sure that Wi-Fi is turned on.

4. Tap the item that represents your network. (If you tap on the blue-circled right arrow next to each network, you can further customize your network settings.)

I Don't Have a Wireless Network

If you don't have a Wi-Fi network but do have high-speed Internet through a telephone or cable provider, you have several options. The first is to call your provider and ask for a new network modem that enables wireless connections. Some providers might upgrade your box for free or a small cost.

Another option is to keep your current box and add a wireless base station of your own, such as the Apple Airport Extreme base station.

5. If the network is protected by a password, you will be asked to enter the password. Once you enter the password, your iPad will remember it. So if you switch between two locations, like work and home, you will be asked to enter the password for each the first time you use that connection. From that point on, your iPad will automatically log on to each connection as you move around.

>>>Go Further

SECURITY? YES!

Your wireless network at home should have security turned on. This means that you should see a padlock next to it in the list of Wi-Fi networks on your iPad. When you select it for the first time, you should be asked to supply a password.

If you don't require a password, seriously consider changing your Wi-Fi network box's settings to add security. The issue isn't simply about requiring a password to use your Internet connection. It is about the fact that a secure network will send encrypted data through the air. Otherwise, anyone can simply "sniff" your wireless connection and see what you are doing online — such as using credit cards and logging on to membership sites. See your network equipment's documentation to set up security.

Setting Up Your 3G Connection

If you have an iPad with 3G capabilities, you can set it up to use AT&T, Verizon, or any other compatible network. You can purchase a monthly data plan or purchase service in shorter increments.

1. Launch the Settings app.

2. Tap Cellular Data on the left.

3. Turn on Cellular Data.

4. Next, you are prompted to create a 3G account with a service. The service will be either AT&T or Verizon in the U.S., depending on which 3G model you own.

5. Enter your name and phone number.

6. Create a username and password.

7. Choose a data plan.

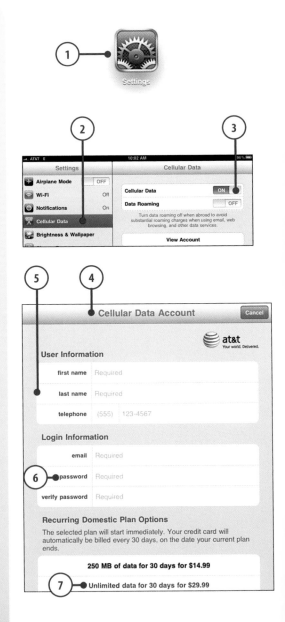

8. Enter your credit card information.

9. Tap Next to proceed through a series of screens to confirm your purchase and approve the license agreement.

10. Tap OK.

Working with Wi-Fi and 3G

After you establish a 3G plan, your iPad should still connect to your Wi-Fi networks when it is in range and use 3G when it cannot find a Wi-Fi network. You can also return to Settings and turn on or off Cellular Data to specifically prevent your iPad from using the 3G network. This is handy when you want to use your iPad on an airplane and are told to turn off all mobile phone devices.

8

Cellular Data Account			Cancel
Payment & Billing Information			

Visa ✓	MasterCard	Discover	Amex

credit card |

name — as it appears on the card

expiration date — MM YYYY

security code — 3 or 4 digits printed on front or back of card

billing address — Address 1

Address 2

City — State — Zip Code

Next

9

Data Plan Activated
Your AT&T cellular data plan has been successfully activated.

10 — OK

It's Not All Good

WATCH FOR DATA ROAMING

In the Cellular Data settings you can turn on or off Data Roaming. This is what enables your iPad to connect to wireless data networks that are outside of your data plan, such as networks in other countries. If you leave Data Roaming on and your iPad connects to such a network, you may find a surprise bill in the mail. You can avoid extra charges by leaving Data Roaming off or by purchasing a plan from AT&T for International data roaming.

Syncing with iTunes

Whether you are on a Mac or PC, you need iTunes to sync your iPad with your computer. If you are on a Mac, you already have iTunes. All you need to do is run Software Update to make sure you have the latest version. If you run Windows, you can get the Windows version of iTunes from Apple's site: http://www.apple.com/itunes/download/.

Now you might be thinking that your iPad is such a great device that it can stand alone. And it can. But if you also use a computer, there are many advantages to syncing your iPad with it.

- Each day you sync your iPad, iTunes stores a backup of its content. You can restore all your data from these backups if you lose your iPad.

- Syncing with a computer is the only way to get a large number of photos from your collection on your iPad.

- Syncing with a computer is the only way to get copies of music you already own, such as music imported from CDs or purchased from stores besides iTunes.

- It can be easier to arrange your app icons on the Home screen pages using iTunes, rather than doing it on your iPad.

- Syncing with iTunes means you can store a large collection of music and video on your computer but choose only a selection of it to appear on your iPad.

- On a Mac in iCal, you have far greater control over setting recurring and special events, which appear on your iPad in the Calendar app, even though you cannot create them there.

You might get a message on your computer the first time you connect your iPad and open iTunes asking if it is okay to sync your iPad to this computer. The message won't reappear.

After connecting to iTunes the first time, all you need to do is connect the iPad to your computer, and iTunes automatically opens. If your iPad has already been connected for a while, you can resync it by clicking the Sync button that appears in iTunes.

Summary button

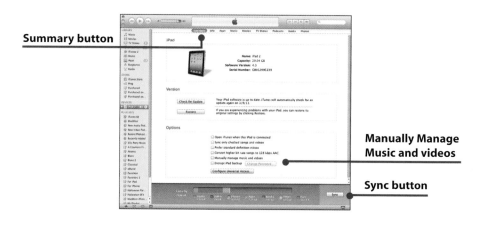

Manually Manage Music and videos

Sync button

After your device is in sync, you can change some general options for your iPad from the Summary screen in iTunes. Most of the options are self-explanatory, such as Open iTunes When the iPad Is Connected.

One option that dramatically changes how your iPad syncs is Manually Manage Music and Videos, which turns off automatic syncing of music and videos and enables you to simply drag and drop songs and movies from your iTunes library onto the iPad icon on the left. (You might need to scroll down the Summary page to locate this checkbox if your screen size is too small to show the entire page at once.)

As we look at some of the syncing options for the iPad, the Mac version of iTunes is used as an example. The Windows version of iTunes is similar but not exactly the same. One difference is that on a Mac, iTunes syncs data with Mac applications such as Address Book, iCal, and iPhoto. On Windows, iTunes must find this data elsewhere.

Syncing Contacts, Calendars, and Other Information

Use the Info page in iTunes to sync your contacts, calendars, and a few other things to your iPad.

1. Click the Info button in iTunes to see options for choosing how to sync your contacts. You can sync all your contacts from Address Book or sync only selected groups.

2. You can also sync with contacts you have stored with either Yahoo! or Google. You need to enter your login information so that iTunes can access the contacts on that service.

3. Choose to sync all the calendars in iCal or just selected ones. In addition, you can choose not to sync old events.

4. Next, you can sync email accounts with Apple's Mail program, which syncs the settings between your computer and your iPad, not the mail messages. See Chapter 8, "Communicating with Email," for more on getting mail on your iPad.

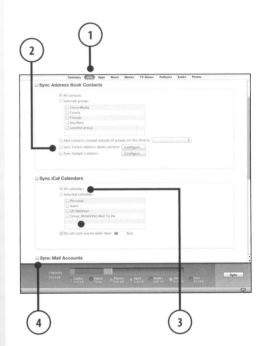

5. To transfer your Mac's bookmarks to your iPad and keep the bookmarks synced between the iPad and the Mac, check the Sync Safari bookmarks check box.

6. Check the Sync notes option to use the Notes app to exchange your iCal and Mail notes between your Mac and the iPad. This is a great way to create notes, lists, and small documents and share them between your iPad and your Mac.

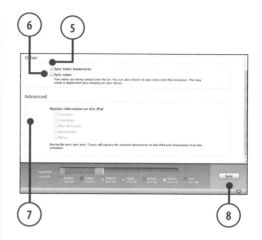

7. Use the Advanced options (Contacts, Calendars, Mail Accounts, Bookmarks, and Notes) to indicate that during the next sync the information should be erased from your iPad and replaced with the corresponding information from your Mac or PC.

8. Click the Sync button to sync.

It's Not All Good

DUPLICATE CALENDARS

If you are already using MobileMe to sync your MobileMe calendar, don't also add it using iTunes. Doing so may give you two copies of all those events: one copy synced over the Internet, and one synced each time you connect to iTunes. Just use MobileMe syncing and leave Sync iCal Calendars unchecked.

Syncing Apps

iTunes keeps your apps on your computer and your iPad in sync and helps you organize them.

Note that you cannot run apps on your computer, just store them. You can store all of the apps you have downloaded and purchased on your computer and only have a subset of those set to sync on to your iPad.

1. Click the Apps button of your iPad's settings in iTunes.

2. Use the list on the left to check or uncheck apps to determine which ones to sync with your iPad.

3. Drag the app icons around on the representation of the Home screen page.

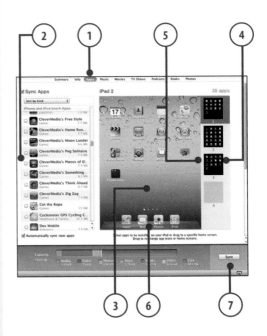

Go Ahead—Select More Than One

You can click more than one app icon in iTunes and then drag them around as groups. This makes it easy to rearrange your apps in iTunes and is the reason many people do it here, rather than on the iPad itself.

4. Select another Home screen page by clicking a page on the right.

5. You can drag an app from the main representation to another page on the right to move it to another page.

6. You can also drag apps in and out of the iPad's dock area at the bottom.

7. Click the Sync button if you want to apply the changes now.

Syncing Documents

Apps sometimes have documents.
For example, Pages is a word processor, so it would naturally have word-
processing documents. Documents
are stored on your iPad, but you
might want to access them on your
Mac or PC as well.

1. Click the Apps button of your
   iPad's settings in iTunes.

2. Scroll down to the bottom of the
   Apps page.

3. In the File Sharing section, choose
   an app.

4. Select a document from the right.

5. Click the Save To button to save
   the document as a file on your
   computer.

6. Click the Add button to import a
   file from your computer to your
   iPad. Each app has its own document space on your iPad. So if you
   have two PDF readers, and you
   want the PDF document available
   to both, you need to add it to
   each app's documents.

No File Sharing Section?

The File Sharing section on the Apps screen will only appear if you have at least
one app that is capable of sharing files through iTunes. Examples would be
Pages, Numbers, Keynote, iMovie, GarageBand, Voice Memos, and GoodReader.

Drag and Drop

You can also use drag and drop to pull documents out of, and import them into,
the app's document space.

Syncing Music

The easy way to sync music is to select Entire Music Library In iTunes on your computer. If you have more music than can fit on your iPad, though, you must make some choices. Syncing Movies, TV Shows, Podcasts, iTunes U, and Books all work in a similar way to syncing music, so you can apply what you learn in these steps to those items as well.

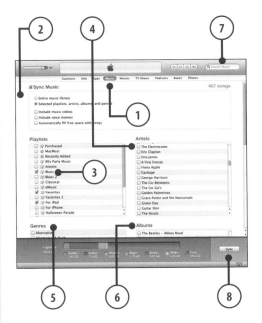

1. Click the Music button of your iPad's settings in iTunes.

2. Click the Selected Playlists, Artists, and Genres button.

3. Check off any playlists in the Playlists section that you want to include.

4. Check off any artists for which you want to include every song by that artist.

5. Check off any genres to include in their entirety.

6. Check off any albums you want to include.

7. Use the search box to quickly find specific artists.

8. Click the Sync button if you want to apply the changes now.

One Copy Only

Note that songs are never duplicated on your iPad. So for instance, if the same song appears in two playlists and is also by an artist that you have selected to sync, the song only has one copy on your iPad. But it appears in both of the playlists and under that artist, album, and alphabetical list of all songs.

>> Go Further

CHECK IT OFF

Another way to select songs to sync with your iPad is to use the Entire Music Library option but also choose Sync Only Checked Songs and Videos from the Summary tab. Then you can pick and choose each song that syncs.

Another option is to strictly use playlists to sync without checking off any artists or genres. Then, in addition to your normal playlists, create one called For iPad and put every song in there that you want on your iPad. Then set that playlist to sync.

Syncing Photos

Syncing your photos actually isn't that much different than syncing music. You can choose to have all your photos transferred to your iPad, or choose them by albums, events, or faces.

1. Click the Photos button of your iPad's settings in iTunes.

2. Click the Sync Photos From check box. If you use iPhoto you should choose iPhoto from the drop-down menu. Other choices for Mac users include choosing any folder or the Pictures folder.

    If you use Windows, you can choose your My Pictures folder or another folder. Any subfolders are treated as albums, and you can select or deselect any of them.

You might sync photos to your iPad by selecting a photo tool, such as a Photoshop Elements, as your sync companion. If you choose that program, you can use the groupings in that program as albums.

3. Choose whether to sync all photos or only selected ones.

4. If you choose selected photos, you can also choose a number of recent events or all events from a recent period of time.

5. Select any albums that you want to sync.

6. Select specific events you want to sync.

7. You can also select to sync all photos tagged for a specific person in iPhoto.

8. Click the Sync button to apply the changes.

No Duplicates

Like with music, you get only one copy of each photo, no matter how many times the photo appears in albums, events, and faces. The photos appear in all the right places but take up only one spot in memory on your iPad.

It's Not All Good

ONE WAY ONLY

Like with the iPhone and iPod touch, syncing photo albums works only one way. For the photos you sync from your computer to your iPad, you cannot pull photos from your iPad back to your computer. Syncing photos from your computer to your iPad works only one way. The original is on your computer, and there is merely a smaller copy on your iPad. So it is important that you maintain your real photo library on your computer and remember to back it up.

Some types of email accounts, such as MobileMe, Google, and Exchange, also store data such as contacts, calendars, and bookmarks, as well as email, which enables multiple devices to keep those things in sync. When you add those kinds of email accounts to your iPad, you will also get the option to sync those kinds of data.

To get MobileMe, check out www.apple.com/mobileme.

Syncing Using MobileMe

If you have a MobileMe account, you can sync parts of your iPad's data wirelessly. You can do it even if your iPad and Mac are not in the same location.

1. Tap the Settings icon on the Home screen and then tap Mail, Contacts, Calendars.

2. Tap Add Account.

3. Tap the MobileMe button.

4. Enter your MobileMe email address and password.

5. Tap Next. It can take a few seconds for your iPad to verify your account.

6. Choose which pieces of data you want to use from your MobileMe account.

7. Enabling Find My iPad lets you to use this feature of MobileMe to locate your iPad if you have lost it or it has been stolen.

8. Tap Save.

Find My iPad Is Free

Even if you are not a MobileMe subscriber, you can still use Find My iPad. All you need is an Apple ID, which would be the same as one you use to buy things from iTunes or log in using Game Center. Use that ID as your MobileMe ID here, and you will be able to enable Find My iPad.

No Email Please

If you do not use your MobileMe email account, you can just switch off Mail in your MobileMe settings. You can still sync the other data and use Find My iPad. Many people choose to use MobileMe for features like bookmark and calendar syncing and don't use their @me.com email addresses for anything.

⑥		⑧
Cancel	MobileMe	Save

✉ Mail	ON
👤 Contacts	OFF
📅 Calendars	OFF
🔖 Bookmarks	ON
📝 Notes	OFF
🌐 Find My iPad	ON

Allow this iPad to be shown on a map or remotely wiped.

⑦

Purchase music and
buy or rent videos.

Play your music and
listen to podcasts.

In this chapter, you learn how to use the iPod and Video apps to play music and watch video.

→ Playing a Song

→ Building a Playlist

→ Purchasing Music

→ Buying and Renting Video

→ Downloading Podcasts

→ Playing Video

→ Playing YouTube Video

→ Using AirPlay to Play Music and Video on Other Devices

Playing Music and Video

The iPad handles playing music as well as any iPod or iPhone ever has, plus it has a big screen for you to use to browse your collection.

Playing a Song

So let's start by simply selecting and playing a song with the iPod app.

1. Tap the iPod icon, which is most likely along the bottom of your Home screen.

2. Tap Music on the left if it isn't already selected.

3. Tap Songs on the bottom if it isn't already selected.

4. Tap the name of a song to start it. At this point the album artwork may expand to fill the screen. If so, tap the screen, and you see the controls appear at the top and other buttons at the bottom. Use the left arrow at the bottom to return to the track list.

5. At the top of the screen, the round Play button changes to a Pause button. The time progress bar under it begins to move.

6. Use the volume slider at the upper left to adjust the volume, or use the physical volume controls.

7. Tap the album art at the bottom left to enlarge it.

8. With the artwork on the screen, tap in the middle to bring back up the play and volume controls, along with the name of the artist, song, and album.

9. Tap the repeat button to make your iPad repeat all songs in the list. Tap the Repeat button a second time to repeat the current song over and over.

10. Tap the Shuffle button to make your iPad play the songs in the list in a random order.

11. Tap the left-facing arrow button at the bottom left to return to the main iPod app interface.

How Else Can I Listen to Music?

You can also listen to music using other third-party apps. Some apps access your music collection on your iPad, but the most interesting ones play streaming music from over the Internet. We look at apps such as Pandora, Rhapsody, and streaming radio apps in Chapter 15, "The World of Apps."

12. Tap any of the buttons at the bottom of the screen—Songs, Artists, Albums, Genres, and Composers—to sort the list of songs.

13. When you sort by albums or genres, you can view a mini-window with the list of songs for any album. Just tap on any album to bring up this list. Tap a song name to play it.

14. Tap in the Search field in the upper right to search your song list.

CONTROLLING MUSIC PLAYBACK

>>> Go Further

To control music playback

- Tap and move the dot in the progress bar at the top of the screen to move around inside a song.

- Use the Back and Forward buttons at the top of the screen to move from song to song in the list of currently selected songs.

- Press the Pause button at any time to pause the music. Use the same button, which has become a Play button, to restart the music.

- When playing a song, tap the album cover at the bottom left to view the album art at full screen, tap the center of the screen to bring up more buttons, and then tap the list button in the lower right to view all the songs on that album.

Building a Playlist

You can create playlists on your Mac or PC in iTunes, but you can also build actual playlists on your iPad.

1. Tap the + button in the bottom-left corner of the main iPod app screen.

2. Give the new playlist a name and tap Save.

Editing Playlists

After you create a playlist, it appears in the Library list on the left side of the main iPod view. Select it and tap the Edit button to remove songs from it, or use the Add Songs button to add more songs.

3. In the expanded list of your music, tap the + buttons next to each song you want to add to the playlist.

4. Tap the Sort buttons at the bottom of the screen to sort through your music.

5. Use the Search field in the upper right to find songs faster.

6. Tap the Done button when you have selected all the songs you want to add to the playlist.

Genius Playlists

If you turn on the Genius feature in your Mac or PC copy of iTunes, you can use the Genius playlist feature to create playlists. After you click the Atom icon, select a song to use as the start of the Genius playlist. iTunes selects other songs from your collection that are similar and creates a playlist using the name of that song.

7. On the playlist edit screen, remove songs from the playlist by tapping on the red buttons.

8. Tap and drag on the three-line buttons to rearrange the songs.

9. Tap Done to complete the playlist. The next time you sync your iPad to iTunes, the new playlist syncs, too.

Making iTunes Purchases

You have lots of options when it comes to adding more music to your iPad. You can simply add more music to your iTunes collection on your computer and then sync those songs to your iPad. In that case, you can buy them from iTunes, from another online source, or import them from music CDs.

How Else Can I Get Music?

You can purchase music on your iPad only through the iTunes app. But you can sync music from your computer that you get from any source that doesn't use special copy protection, like CDs you import into iTunes. You can buy online from places such as Amazon.com, eMusic.com, AmieStreet.com, or even directly from the websites of some artists.

In addition to syncing music to your iPad from your computer, you can purchase music, movies, TV shows, and audio books directly on your iPad using the iTunes app and using the same account that you use in iTunes on your computer.

1. Tap the iTunes app icon on your Home screen to go to the iTunes store.

2. Use the buttons at the top of the screen to choose from today's Featured selections or the Top Charts, or build a Genius list based on music you already own.

3. Tap the left and right arrows on the middle section to browse more featured albums.

4. Use the Search field at the top to search for an artist, album, or song by name.

5. Select a suggestion from the list, or tap the Search button on the keyboard to complete the search.

6. Find an album you want to buy, and tap its artwork to view more information.

Syncing Devices

After you make an iTunes purchase, the music, TV show, or movie you downloaded should transfer to your computer the next time you sync your iPad. From your computer, you can sync your new purchase to any other device you use that uses your iTunes account.

7. Tap a song name to listen to a sample of the song.

8. Tap outside of the album window to close it and return to the previous view.

9. To buy the album, tap the price of the album and then tap again on the Buy Album button.

10. You can also tap the price of a song to purchase just that song.

How About My Home Videos?

If you shoot a home video with a video camera, or iPod Nano or iPhone, you can bring that into iTunes on your Mac or PC and sync it to your iPad. They appear as Movies, right next to your purchased content.

What About My DVDs?

If you can import CD music content into iTunes, you'd think you'd be able to import video content from your DVDs. Well, technically it is possible (although not necessarily legal) by using programs like Handbrake (http://handbrake.fr/) for your Mac or PC to import DVD content and then drag the resulting file into iTunes. Then you can sync it with your iPad.

BUYING AND RENTING VIDEO

>> Go Further

Although the process of buying video is essentially the same as buying music, some significant details are different. It is worth taking a look at these details so that you know what you are getting into before spending your money.

Copy Protection   Although music in the iTunes store recently became copy-protection free, videos are a different story altogether. Purchased videos can be played back only on the Apple devices you own that use your iTunes account. You can't burn videos to a DVD, for instance, or watch them on a TV unless it is hooked up to an Apple device. Rentals are even more strict because you can watch them only on the device you rent them on.

Collecting Movies   Thinking of starting a collection of videos by purchasing them from Apple? Keep in mind that these videos take up a lot of space on your hard drive. An iPad, even a 64GB version, quickly fills up if you start adding dozens of movies. Also keep in mind that the file formats used for these movies is relatively new, and you might not be able to play them in 5 or 10 years.

Time-Delayed Rentals   Rentals have some strict playback restrictions. After you download a rental, you have 30 days to watch it. After you start watching it, you have only 24 hours to finish it.

TV Show Season Passes   You can purchase seasons of TV shows that aren't complete yet. When you do this, you are basically pre-ordering each episode. You get the existing episodes immediately but have to wait for the future episodes. They usually appear the next day after airing on network television.

Multi-Pass   In addition to season passes, you can also get a Multi-Pass, which is for TV shows that broadcast daily. When you purchase a Multi-Pass, you get the most recent episode of the show plus the next 15 episodes when they become available.

HD Versus SD   You can purchase or rent most movies and TV shows in either HD (high definition) or SD (standard definition). The difference is the quality of the image, which affects the file size, of course. If you have a slow connection or limited bandwidth, you might want to stick to SD versions of the shows.

Downloading Podcasts

Podcasts are episodic shows, either audio or video, produced by major networks, small companies, and single individuals. You'll find news, information, tutorials, music, comedy, drama, talk shows, and more. There is something covering almost any topic you can think of.

1. Tap the iTunes app icon on your Home screen.

2. Tap the Podcasts button at the bottom of the screen.

3. Tap Top Charts to see the top podcasts divided into audio and video podcasts. At the bottom of the lists you see a "Show More" button that you can tap to add more to each list.

4. Tap the Categories button to view all podcast categories.

5. Select a category to view featured podcasts for that category.

6. Tap the Search field to enter a search term. You can search for a podcast title or topic. Search results show podcasts and other iTunes content that matches the search term.

7. Tap a podcast to view more information about it.

8. Tap the Free button next to each episode to download the episode and add it to your iPod collection. A downloaded podcast appears under Podcast in your library.

9. Because the iPod app plays back only audio, if you select a video podcast you will automatically launch the Videos app. This can get a little confusing because when the video is done or you press the Done button, you end up in the Videos app, not the iPod app.

What About Subscribing?

Unfortunately the iPad cannot subscribe to podcasts on its own. Podcasts, being episodic, are meant to be subscribed to so that you automatically get new episodes. To use your iPad to follow an episodic podcast, subscribe to it on your computer, and then sync to your iPad to get new episodes.

MacMost

MacMost Now - Mac and iPhone Tips and Tutorials

Tell a Friend >

Category: Software How-To
Language: English
★★★★★ 200 Ratings

Podcast Description

Get the most from your Mac, iPhone, iPod and Apple TV! The video podcast features tips, tricks, techniques, tutorials and reviews geared toward the casual personal and business Apple user.

Website >

Tap to Preview

	Name	Price
1	MacMost Now 524: Password Protected Documents	FREE
2	MacMost Now 523: iPad 2: Faster, Thinner, Lighter, Plus Cameras	FREE
3	MacMost Now 522: Text Selection Shortcuts	FREE
4	MacMost Now 521: What Is Thunderbolt?	FREE
5	MacMost Now 520: Cutting Out Objects In Images Using Preview	FREE
6	MacMost Now 519: Hyperlinks In iWork Pages	FREE

Playing Video

After you have movies, TV shows, and Podcast videos on your iPad, you need to play them using the Videos app.

1. Tap the Videos icon on your Home screen.

2. The Movies you have on your iPad display by default. Tap TV Shows or Podcasts to switch lists. If you don't have videos in one or more of these categories, then that button may not appear at all.

3. Tap a movie to view more information about it.

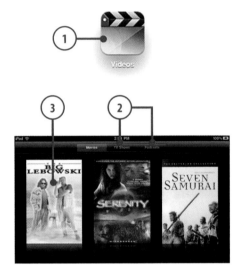

Any Video Alternatives to Apple?

You bet. An app for Netflix launched with the iPad that Netflix subscribers can use to rent movies. Some companies, such as ABC, have also provided their own apps for viewing their shows on the iPad. You can also view video from any site that has video in standard MP4 formats. The site www.archive.org/details/movies has public domain movies and videos, often in MP4 format. The popular video site http://blip.tv also works well with the iPad.

4. Tap the Play button to start the movie.

5. Tap the Chapters button to view a list of chapters in the movie.

6. After a movie is playing, tap in the middle of the screen to bring up the controls.

7. Tap the Done button to exit the movie and return to the movie information screen.

8. Tap the Pause button to pause the movie and then again to resume.

9. Adjust the volume with the volume control.

10. Drag the dot along the line to move to a different section of the movie.

11. Use the Back and Forward buttons to jump between chapters.

12. Use the AirPlay button to send the video stream to another device, such as an Apple TV. See "Using AirPlay To Play Music and Video on Other Devices" later in this chapter.

Changing the Orientation

For most video content you can rotate your iPad to view in a horizontal orientation and use the Zoom button at the upper right to crop the left and right sides of the video so that it fits vertically on the screen. This is similar to watching a movie on a standard TV.

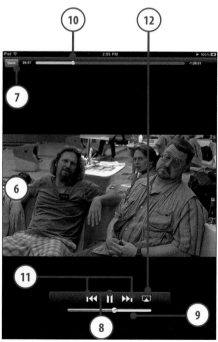

Viewing YouTube Videos

It isn't all about professionally produced movies and TV shows anymore. You might also want to use your iPad to watch poor-quality videos of cats playing pianos and kids lip-syncing to pop songs.

Fortunately, the YouTube app comes with your iPad. You can browse and play most, if not all, of the video at the most popular video site on the Web.

1. Tap the YouTube icon on your Home screen.

Do I Need a YouTube Account?

You don't need a YouTube account to view videos. However, with a free online account, you can keep track of your favorites, subscribe to channels, and leave comments and ratings.

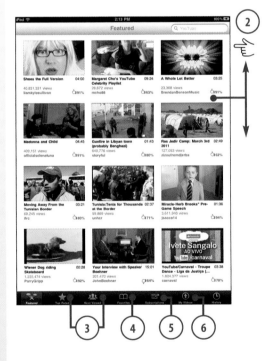

2. The Featured page of YouTube displays. Scroll up and down by dragging.

3. Tap the Top Rated and Most Viewed buttons to see other lists. You can sort those lists by Today, This Week, or All.

4. Tap Favorites to go to a page that lists your favorite videos and playlists after you signed in.

5. Tap Subscriptions to see the video channels that you subscribe to.

6. Tap My Videos button to see a list of the videos you have uploaded to your account.

7. Tap the History button to see a list of the videos you most recently viewed.

8. Tap on a video on any screen to play the video. Rotating your iPad plays the video full screen.

9. The video plays with controls at the top and bottom of the video. You might need to tap in the center of the video to bring up the controls.

10. Tap the Play/Pause button to start and stop the video.

11. Tap the buttons at the top of the video to add a video to your list of favorites, share a video link via email, rate a video, or flag it.

12. Tap the double arrow button to expand the playback to full screen.

13. Tap the buttons at the bottom of the video to switch between views of video information, related videos, more videos from the same channel, and comments.

14. Tap the Comments button, and then tap Add a Comment to type your own comment.

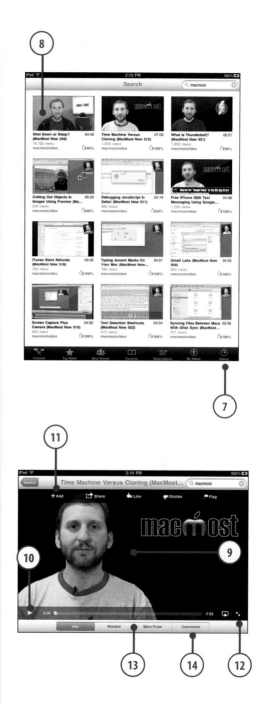

Using AirPlay to Play Music and Video on Other Devices

In iTunes, with the Video app and many other apps that play music or video, you have the option to send the audio or video stream from your iPad to another device that is connected to the same Wi-Fi network, such as an Apple TV.

You need to enable AirPlay on those devices first. For instance, using the Apple TV 2 you need to go into settings on the device and turn on AirPlay. You also need to make sure that the device is using the same Wi-Fi network as your iPad.

1. Look for the AirPlay button in the app you are using. Tap it to bring up a list of available devices.

2. Your iPad will show as the first device. Use this to switch back to playing the media on your iPad if you have switched to something else.

3. Next to each device you will see either a screen icon or a speaker icon. This tells you whether you can stream video or just audio using that device.

4. Tap on another device, and the music or video currently playing will start to play over that device.

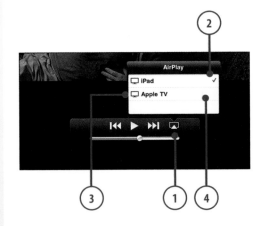

Home Sharing

You can also stream music and video the other way. If you are using iTunes on your Mac or PC you can play this iTunes content on your iPad if it is on the same local network.

1. In iTunes on your Mac or PC, choose Turn On Home Sharing from the Advanced menu. You are prompted to enter your Apple account ID and password.

2. In the Settings App, choose iPod settings.

3. Enter the same Apple account ID and password.

4. In the iPod app, tap the Library heading at the top of the list on the left.

5. Tap the name of the library you want to access. The content in your iPod app changes to reflect the content in the iTunes library on your Mac or PC. You can now play songs from your computer without having to transfer them to your iPad first.

How About Video?

After you have Home Sharing working in the iPod app, you should notice that it also works in the Videos app. Next to Movies, TV Shows and Podcasts, you will see a Shared category at the top of the screen. Tap that to select a shared library and view video content that you can stream to your iPad.

It's Not All Good

WHAT IF MY LIBRARY DOESN'T APPEAR?

Home Sharing is tricky. It requires that you use the same iTunes account IDs on both your iPad and on your Mac or PC. It also requires that you have the iPad on the same local network as your Mac or PC. In addition, network firewalls and other software may get in the way. It usually works effortlessly, but some users have reported trouble getting Home Sharing to work at all with their particular home network setup.

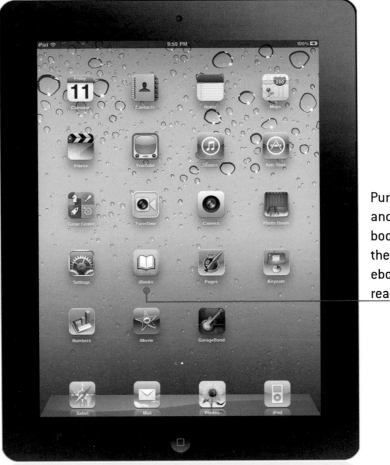

Purchase and read books with the iPad's ebook reader.

Find out how to purchase books from the iBooks store and how to read them on your iPad.

→ Buying a Book from Apple

→ Reading a Book

→ Using Reading Aids

→ Adding Notes and Highlights

→ Adding Bookmarks

→ Organizing Your Books

→ Using iBooks Alternatives

Reading Books

We finally have a better way to enjoy books. As an ebook reader, your iPad can give you access to novels and textbooks alike, storing hundreds inside and allowing you to purchase more right from the device.

A single app, the iBooks app, allows you to both read and purchase new books. You can also download and add books from other sources.

Buying a Book from Apple

The first thing to do with the iBooks app is to get some books! You can buy books using the store in the app. You can also find some free books there.

1. Tap the iBooks app icon to launch iBooks.

2. Tap the Store button to switch to the iBooks store.

Don't Want to Purchase from Apple?

You don't necessarily need to buy books from Apple. You can buy from any seller that sends you an ePub or PDF formatted file with no copy protection. After you have the file, just drag and drop it into iTunes. It will add it to your books collection there, ready to be synced to your iPad.

3. Tap one of the four arrows to scroll left and right through the featured books.

4. Tap See All to go to a list of the featured books.

5. Tap the Categories button to bring up a list of categories.

6. Tap a category to go to a list of featured books in that category, or drag in the list to scroll up and down.

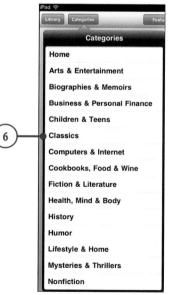

7. Tap any book cover to view more information about the book.

8. Tap the price next to a book to purchase it.

9. The price button changes to Buy Book. Tap it again to continue with the purchase.

10. Tap the Get Sample button to download a sample of the book.

Reading a Book

Reading books is a simple process. Following are the basics of reading your downloaded books.

1. Tap the iBooks app icon to launch iBooks.

2. Tap a book to open it.

3. To turn a page, tap and hold any-where along the right side of the page, and drag to the left. A vir-tual page turns.

4. Tap and drag from the left to the right or simply tap the left side of the page to turn the page back.

5. To move quickly through pages, tap and drag the small marker at the bottom of the page along the dotted line. Release to jump to a page.

6. Tap the Table of Contents button at the top to view a table of contents.

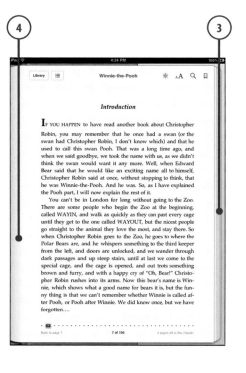

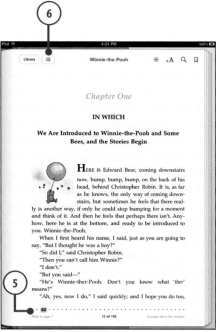

7. Tap anywhere in the table of contents to jump to that part of the book.

8. Tap the Resume button to return to the page you were previously viewing.

9. Tap the Library button to return to your books. If you return to the book later, you return to the last page you viewed.

Tired of the Special Effects?

If you tire of the page-turning special effect, a quick tap on the right or left side of the screen also turns pages. The effect still shows, but it's quick.

Using Reading Aids

iBooks has a variety of ways you can customize your reading experience. You can change the font size, the font itself, and even turn your iPad on its side to see two pages at one time.

1. While viewing a page in iBooks, tap the brightness control at the top of the screen.

2. Drag the brightness control left or right. Dragging to the left makes the screen dim, which you might use if you're reading in a dark room. Dragging to the right makes it bright, which could make reading easier while outdoors.

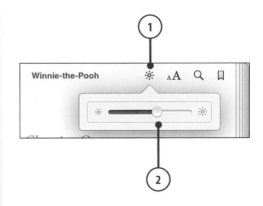

3. Tap the Font adjustment button at the top of the screen.

4. Tap the smaller "A" button to reduce the size of the text.

5. Tap the larger "A" button to increase the size of the text.

6. Tap the Sepia button to change the page color from white to beige.

7. Tap the Fonts button to choose from a few font options.

8. Tap one of the fonts to select it.

9. Turn your iPad on its side to change to a two-page view. (Make sure your orientation lock is not on.)

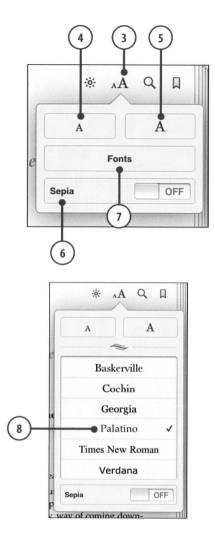

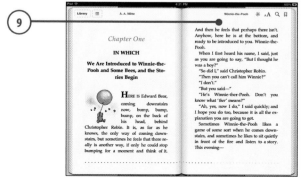

Where Did the Buttons Go?

If you tap in the middle of the screen, the buttons at the top and the dotted line at the bottom disappear. You can still turn the pages; you just don't have access to these buttons. To see the buttons again, tap in the middle of the screen.

Adding Notes and Highlights

Each time you launch iBooks, your iPad returns you to the page you were last reading. However, you might want to mark a favorite passage or a bit of key information.

1. Go to a page in a book in iBooks.

2. Tap a word and hold your finger there until a magnifying glass appears.

3. Release your finger and you see four choices: Dictionary, Highlight, Note, and Search.

Dictionary and Search

Tapping Dictionary brings up a definition of the word. Tapping Search brings up a list of the locations of the word throughout the text.

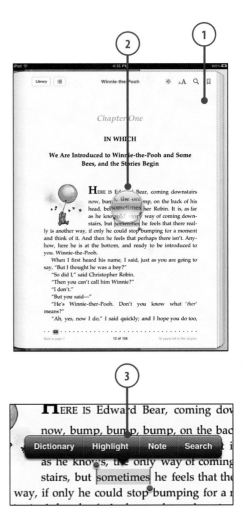

4. Drag the blue dots to enlarge the section of text highlighted.

5. Tap Highlight.

6. The text highlight now changes color. Tap the text again to see a set of choices that enables you to choose a different color.

7. Tap a color or tap Remove Highlight to remove the color. You can use different colors to represent different things. For instance, if you are marking passages in a textbook, you can highlight important facts with one color and points that you want to research in the future with another color.

8. Tap Note instead of Highlight to bring up a yellow pad of paper and add a note.

9. Tap in the note to bring up the keyboard and start typing.

10. Tap outside the yellow paper to finish the note. It will then appear as a small yellow sticky note to the right side of the page. Tap it any time you want to view or edit the note. You can delete a note by removing all text in the note.

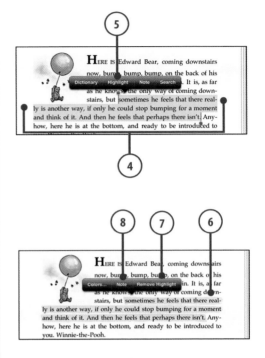

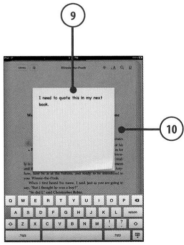

Adding Bookmarks

You can also bookmark a page to easily find it later.

1. Tap the bookmark button at the top of a page to bookmark the page. You can bookmark as many pages as you want in a book.

2. Tap it again to remove the bookmark from the page.

3. Tap the table of contents button to go to the table of contents.

4. Tap the Bookmarks button at the top of the table of contents to see a list of all the bookmarks, highlights, and notes you have added to the book.

5. Tap any bookmark, note, or highlight to jump to it.

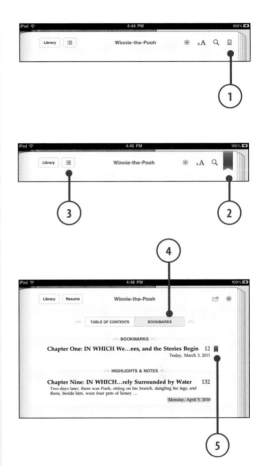

Organizing Your Books

Like to read a lot? You aren't alone. I'm sure many people gather massive collections of ebooks on their iPads. Fortunately, iBooks includes a few ways to organize your ebooks.

1. Go to your iBooks main page—your Library.

2. Tap the Collections button.

3. Tap a Collection name to jump to that collection. Think of collections as different bookcases filled with books.

4. Tap New to create a new collection.

5. Tap Edit to delete or re-order collections in the list.

6. Tap the Edit button to enter edit mode.

7. Tap one or more books to select them.

8. Tap the Move button to move those books to another collection.

9. Tap the Delete button to delete those books.

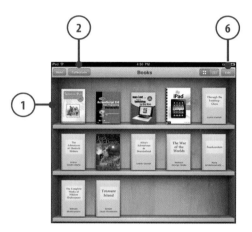

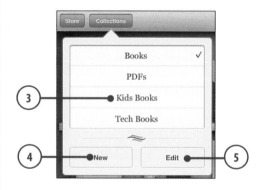

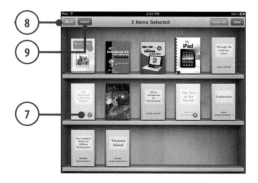

10. Tap and hold your finger over a book to drag it to a new position in the library. You can also do this in normal mode or in edit mode.

11. Tap Done to exit edit mode.

12. Tap the List View button.

13. Now you can see a vertical list of your books. Scroll up and down by dragging and flicking.

14. Tap the Titles, Authors, and Categories buttons at the bottom of the screen to change the order of the list.

15. Use the search field to search your library. If you don't see a search field, tap and drag down on the whole list to reveal it. You can also drag down the screen to reveal the search box in the normal icon view of books and type in a search keyword there.

Another Way to Delete

You can also delete books in list view by swiping from left to right across the title of a book. A Delete button appears to the right. Tap it to delete the book.

Using iBooks Alternatives

Copy protection prevents you from taking your ebooks from one platform to the other. Thankfully there are Kindle and Nook apps for the iPad, so you can read the books you purchase from those stores.

1. When you launch the Kindle app, you see a screen that displays your library. Tap a book to open it.

2. Tap the Font button to change the font size.

3. Tap the bookmark button to add bookmarks and jump to a new page.

Track your
appointments
and events.

Take notes and
create lists.

Store and
search
all your
contacts.

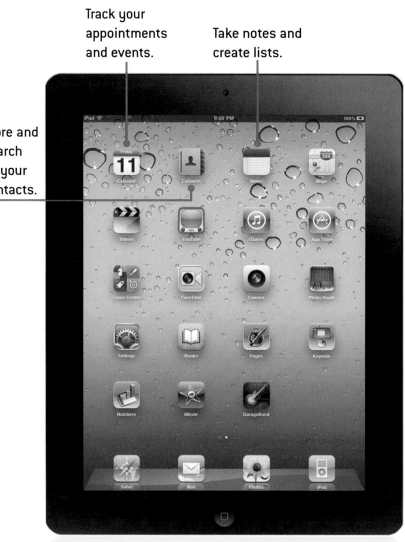

In this chapter we learn how to add and look up contacts and calendar events. We also look at the Notes app.

→ Adding a Contact

→ Searching for a Contact

→ Working with Contacts

→ Creating a Calendar Event

→ Using Calendar Views

→ Creating Notes

Organizing Your Life

If you have many friends and get invited to lots of parties, you can use the iPad to organize your life with the default Contacts and Calendar apps. Let's take a close look at some of the things you can do with these apps.

Adding a Contact

If you use Address Book on your Mac or the equivalent on Windows, all your contacts can transfer to your iPad the first time you sync. However, you can also add contacts directly on your iPad.

1. Tap the Contacts app icon to launch the app.

2. Press the + button near the bottom of the screen. A New Contact form and a keyboard appears.

3. Type the first name of the contact. No need to use Shift to capitalize the name because that happens automatically.

4. Tap the return key on the keyboard to advance to the next field.

5. Continue to type data into fields and tap return. Tap return to skip any fields you don't want to fill.

6. Tap Add Photo to add a photo from one of your photo albums.

Don't Worry About Formatting

You don't need to type phone numbers with parentheses or dashes. Your iPad formats the number for you.

7. Tap the green + button next to Add New Address to add a physical address to the contact.

8. Tap the green + button next to Add Field to add a field such as a middle name, job title, birthday, and so on.

9. Tap the name of a field you would like to add. Or tap away from the pop-up menu to dismiss it.

10. Tap the Done button to complete the new contact.

Contacts that you add to your iPad sync back to your computer the next time you connect. If you have the MobileMe service, the contact should sync across all your MobileMe-enabled devices within minutes if your iPad and those devices are connected to the Internet.

Searching for a Contact

If you didn't have a lot of friends before, I'm sure you gained quite a few since you became the first on your block to own an iPad. So how do you search though all those contacts to find the one you want?

1. Tap the Contacts app icon to launch the app.

2. Tap in the Search field. A keyboard appears at the bottom of the screen.

Other Ways to Find Contacts

You can also drag (or flick to move quickly) through the contact list to find a name. In addition, the list of letters on the left side of the Contacts app enables you to jump right to that letter in your contacts list.

3. Start typing the name of the person you are looking for. As soon as you start typing, the app starts making a list of contacts that contain the letters you've typed.

4. Keep typing until you narrow down the list of names and spot the one you are looking for.

5. Tap the name to bring up the contact.

6. Tap the X button to dismiss the search.

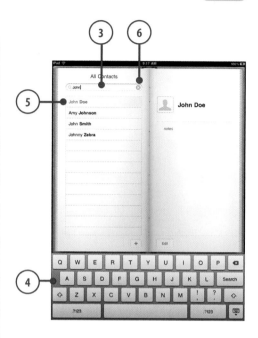

Working with Contacts

After you have contacts in your iPad, you can do a few things from a contact in the Contacts app.

1. Tap and hold the name to copy it to the clipboard buffer.

2. Tap and hold the phone number to copy it to the clipboard buffer.

3. Tap the email address to start composing a new email in the Mail app.

4. Tap to the right of Notes to add more information without entering Edit mode.

5. Tap Edit to enter Edit mode, which gives you the same basic functionality as entering a new contact.

6. Tap Share to start a new email message with a vcard version of the contact.

7. This is the space for an image. To add an image, enter Edit mode by tapping the Edit button at the bottom of the page, and then tapping this space.

8. Tap FaceTime to start a video call (see Chapter 10).

9. Tap Add to Favorites to add to your FaceTime favorites list.

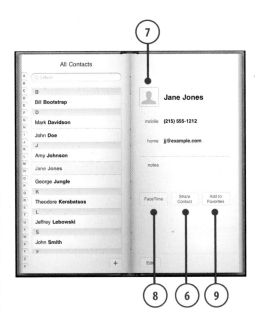

Creating a Calendar Event

Now that you have people in your Contacts app, you need to schedule some things to do with them. Let's look at the Calendar app.

1. Tap the Calendar app icon on the Home screen.

2. Tap the + button at the bottom right.

3. Enter a title for the event.

4. Enter a Location for the event, or skip this field.

5. Tap the Starts/Ends area to bring up date controls.

6. Drag the day, hour, minute, and AM/PM wheels to set the start time for the event.

7. Tap Ends.

8. Drag the day, hour, minute, and AM/PM wheels to set the end time for the event.

9. If the event is an all-day event, turn on the All-Day switch.

10. Tap Done to complete entering the time for the event.

11. Tap Repeat to select a repeating cycle for the event.

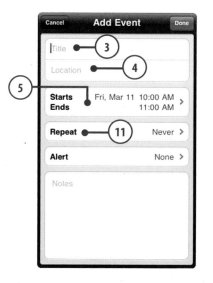

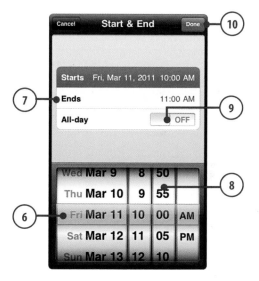

12. Tap the frequency of the event, or leave it at None for a single occurrence.

13. Tap Done to return to the main event screen.

14. Tap Alert to enter an alert time for the event.

15. Select how much time before the event you want the alert to sound.

16. Tap Done to return to the main event screen.

17. Tap in the Notes field and type any additional information for the event.

18. Tap Done to complete the event.

Using Calendar Views

There are four different ways to view your calendar: Day, Week, Month, and List. Let's take a look at each.

Day View

The daily view is broken into two halves: a list of the events scheduled for the day and a scrolling area with a block for each half-hour.

You can tap and drag the right area to move up and down in the day. Above that area is a space for all-day events, if there are any.

The month calendar at the upper right enables you to jump to another day in your schedule by tapping a date. You can also choose a date by tapping and sliding the bar at the bottom of the screen, or jump to the previous or next month by tapping the abbreviated month name.

Move one day at a time through the calendar by tapping the arrows at the bottom of the screen. The Today button takes you to the current day's schedule.

You can tap an event on either side of the page to view details and edit it.

Week View

Current Day

Current Time

Event Detail

Event

Add Event

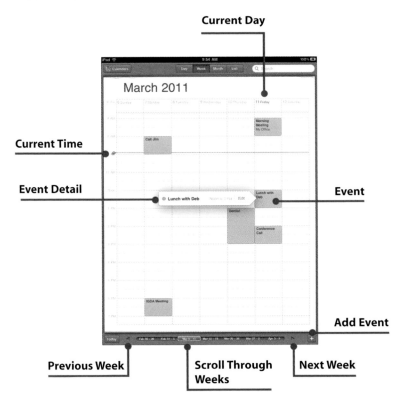

Previous Week

Scroll Through Weeks

Next Week

The Week view is a grid. It shows you Sunday through Saturday of the current week. Each event is shown in the grid, and you can tap on one to see its full title, location, and time.

The red dot and line indicates the current time, and the name of the current day is blue at the top of the screen. Use the line at the bottom of the screen to navigate to previous or upcoming weeks.

Month View

Current Day

Event Detail

Event

Add Event

Previous Year

Scroll Through Months

Next Year

The Month view provides a large view of events. It is still a grid but in a traditional monthly view, with the days from the previous and next months filling in the extra blocks.

Each block lists the events scheduled for that day. You can tap on one to get more information or edit it.

The line at the bottom of the screen changes to a monthly timeline, with previous and next years also listed so that you can jump from year to year.

List View

Selected Event
Information

Event List

Selected Event

Day List

Jump to Today's
Schedule

Add Event

Previous Day

Scroll
Through
Days

Next Day

Jump to the
Previous Month

Jump to the
Next Month

The List view is an interesting combination of things. On the left you get a list of all your events, not just the ones for the current day. You can scroll forward even more if you want to see what is coming up.

On the right, you get a daily timeline like the Day view. But instead of a month calendar at the time, you get information about the currently selected event.

Creating Notes

Another organization app that comes with your iPad is the Notes app. Although this one is much more free-form than a Contacts or Calendar app, it can be useful for keeping quick notes or to-do lists.

1. Tap the Notes icon on your Home screen.

2. Notes opens up the note you were previously working on. To type, tap on the screen where you want the insertion poin, and a keyboard appears.

What's in a Name

The filename for a note is just the first line of the note, so get in the habit of putting the title of a note as the first line of text to make finding the note easier.

3. To start a new note, tap the + button at the upper right.

4. To view a list of all your notes, and to jump to another note, tap the Notes button.

5. Tap the name of the note you want to switch to.

6. Tap and type in the Search field to find text inside of notes.

7. Turn your iPad to horizontal orientation, and the Notes button is replaced with a permanent list of notes on the left.

8. Tap the arrow buttons at the bottom of the screen to jump between notes.

9. Tap the Mail button at the bottom of the screen to start a new email message in the Mail app using the contents of the note.

10. Tap the Trash button at the bottom to delete notes.

Notes Isn't a Word Processor

You can't actually use Notes for any serious writing. There aren't any styles or formatting choices. You can't even change the display font to make it larger. If you need to use your iPad for writing, consider Pages or a third-party word processing app.

>>> Go Further

MULTIPLE NOTES ACCOUNTS

What happens to notes after you create them can be confusing. Notes usually are attached to email accounts in the same way email messages are. So creating a new note can make it appear in your email inbox like it is a new message. You can usually adjust what appears in an "inbox" in your email account settings. Sometimes you can specify that you don't want to see notes there. It depends on your email provider.

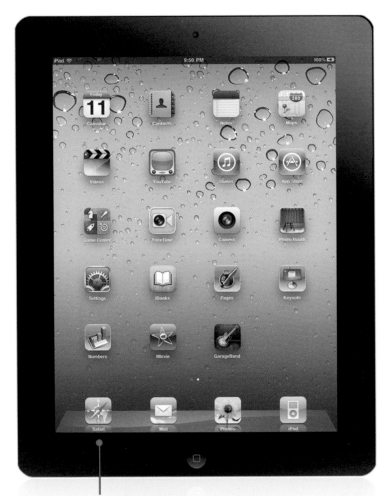

The Web is at your fingertips
with iPad's Safari Web browser.

In this chapter you learn about Safari, the browser built-in to the iPad. You can use it to browse the Web, bookmark web pages, fill in forms, and search the Internet.

→ Configuring Safari Settings
→ Browsing the Web

Surfing the Web

The iPad is a beautiful web surfing device. Its size is perfect for web pages, and your ability to touch the screen lets you interact with content in a way that even a computer typically cannot.

If you have been using the iPhone or the iPod touch to browse the Web, you immediately notice how you no longer have to pinch and rotate to read text or see links. The screen size is much more ideal for web pages than a mobile phone device.

Browsing to a URL

Undoubtedly, you know how to get to web pages on a computer using a web browser. You use Safari on your iPad in the same way, but the interface is a little different.

At the top of the Safari browser is a toolbar with just a few buttons. In the middle, the largest interface element is the address field. This is where you can type the address of any web page on the Internet.

1. Touch the Safari icon on your iPad to launch the browser. It might be located at the bottom of the screen, along with your other most commonly used applications.

2. Tap in the address field at the top of the screen. This opens up the keyboard at the bottom of the screen. If you were already viewing a web page, the address of that page remains in the address field. Otherwise, it will be blank.

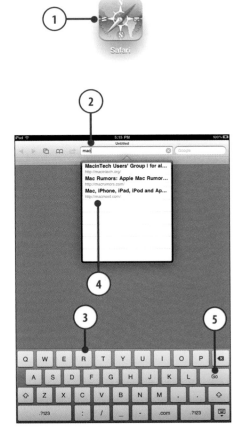

Clear the Slate

To clear the field at any time, tap the X button located inside the field all the way to the right.

3. Start typing a URL such as apple.com or macmost.com.

4. As you type, suggestions based on previous pages you have visited appear. To go directly to one of these pages, tap the page's address in the list.

5. Tap the Go button on the keyboard when you finish typing.

TIPS FOR TYPING A URL

- A URL is a Universal Resource Locator. It can be a website name or a specific page in a website.

- For most websites, you don't need to type the "www." at the beginning. For instance, you can type **www.apple.com** or **apple.com** and both take you to Apple's home page. You never need to type "http://" either, though occasionally you need to type "https://" to specify that you want to go to a secure web page.

- Instead of typing ".com." you can tap the .com button on the iPad keyboard. If you tap and hold the .com button, you can select .edu, .org, or .net as well.

Nothing Special, Please

Some websites present you with a special iPad version of the site. This is not as common as the special iPhone or iPod Touch versions that many sites offer. If a website does not look the same on your iPad as it does on your computer, you might want to check to see if a switch is on the web page provided by the site to view the standard web version, instead of a special iPad version. This is especially useful if a site has lumped the iPad together with the iPhone and provided a needlessly simplified version.

Searching the Web

The Web wouldn't be useful if you had to already know the exact location of every web page to view it. The iPad's Safari web browser has search built into it, as a field right at the top of the screen.

As you type, Safari suggests search terms based on previous searches that others have performed starting with the same characters. This list, which changes as you type, can save you a lot of time and even help you better define what you are looking for.

1. Open Safari and tap in the search field at the upper-right portion. It expands, shrinking the address field to give it more room. The keyboard pops up at the bottom of the screen.

2. Start typing your search term.

3. As you type, a pop-up list appears with suggestions. You can stop typing at any time and tap one of these suggestions to select it and start the search.

4. Tap the X button to the right of the search field at any time to clear the field. If you previously searched for something, it might have appeared in the field when you started your search, and you can use the X button to clear that text.

5. Tap the Search button on the keyboard to finish the text entry and start the search.

6. The results display in a typical Google search results page. Tap any link to go to a page, or use the links at the bottom of the screen to view more results.

Search This Page

Below Google Suggestions in the search suggestions drop-down menu is a list of recent searches and the occurrences of the phrase on the web page you are viewing. Use the latter to find the phrase on the page.

TIPS FOR SEARCHING THE WEB

You can go deeper than just typing some words. For instance, you can put a + in front of a word to require it and a − in front to avoid that word in the results.

You can use special search terms to look for things such as movie times, weather, flight tracking, and more. See http://www.google.com/landing/searchtips/ for all sorts of things you can do with a Google search.

Using iPad's Settings app, you can choose the search engine that Safari uses as its default. Tap the Settings icon and choose Safari on the left, and then look for the Search Engine setting. You can choose Yahoo! instead of Google, for instance.

Using Google, you can search for much more than text on web pages. Look at the top of the search results, and you see links such as Images, Videos, Maps, News, and Shopping. Tap "more" and you can also search for things such as Blogs and Books.

To explore the search results without moving away from the page listing the results, tap and hold over a link to see a button that enables you to open a link in a new page, leaving the results open in the current page.

You can use many search settings with Google. These are not specific to the iPad but work on your computer as well when performing searches. Tap the Search Settings link in the upper-right corner of the search results page to choose a language, filters, and other settings. Set up a Google account (same as a gmail account) and log in to save these search preferences and use them between different devices.

Viewing Web Pages

Whether you typed in a URL or searched for a web page, after you have one open on your iPad screen, you can control what you view in several ways. You need to know these techniques to view the complete contents of a web page and navigate among web pages.

1. Navigate to any web page using either of the two techniques in the previous step-by-step instructions.

2. When you are viewing a page, you can touch and drag the page up and down with your finger. As you do so, notice the bar on the right side that gives you an indication of how much of the complete web page you are viewing at one time.

Flick It

If you release your finger from the iPad screen to stop scrolling while dragging, the screen will continue to scroll with a decelerating affect and then come to a stop quickly.

3. To zoom in on an area in the page, touch the screen with two fingers and move your fingers apart. This is called an unpinch. You can also move them closer together (pinch) to zoom back out. A double-tap restores the page to normal scaling.

4. You can also double-tap images and paragraphs of text to zoom in to those elements in the web page. A second double-tap zooms back out.

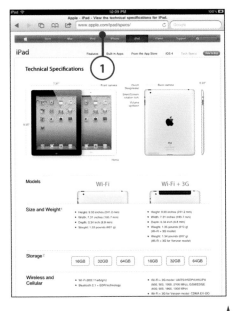

5. While zoomed in, you can also touch and drag left and right to view different parts of the web page. You see a bar at the bottom of the screen when you do this, just like the bar on the right side in step 2.

6. To move to another web page from a link in the current web page, just tap the link. Links are usually an underlined or colored piece of text; however, they can also be pictures or button-like images.

It's Not All Good

WHERE'S THE LINK?

Unfortunately it isn't always easy to figure out which words on a page are links. Years ago, these were all blue and underlined. But today links can be any color and may not be underlined.

On the iPad it is even more difficult to figure out which words are links. This is because many web pages highlight links when the cursor moves over the word. But with the touch interface of the iPad, there is no cursor.

Returning to Previously Visited Websites

Returning to the last page you visited is easy. Just tap the Back button, which is the left-facing triangle at the top-left corner of the Safari screen. You can continue to tap the Back button to go to pages you visited previously.

Likewise, you can tap the button next to it, the Forward button, to reverse your direction and move forward, returning to your more recently viewed pages.

A more precise way to view previous pages is to use the History button.

1. After using Safari to view several pages, tap the Bookmarks/History button at the top of the screen.

2. A list of pages that you visited today appears. If this list is long, you can tap and drag up and down to scroll through the results. If you don't see your history, tap on History to go there. Or, tap the button to the left of the menu title to return to the topmost menu and then press History.

3. Tap any item in the list to jump to that web page.

4. If you visited many sites today, Earlier Today appears and below that, previous days may also appear. Tap to dig down into the history for that date.

5. When you are into the history for a specific date, you can tap and drag to scroll up and down on longer lists, or tap an item to jump to that page.

6. You can move back up from a specific date to the main History menu by tapping the History button at the top-left part of the History pop-up menu.

History/Bookmarks

Safari treats both History and Bookmarks the same. They are both just lists of web pages. Think of your history as a bookmark list of every site you have visited recently.

>>> Go Further

TIPS FOR USING HISTORY

- You can clear your history at any time by tapping the Clear History button at the top of the History pop-up menu.

- You can close the History pop-up menu by tapping the History button again or tapping anywhere else on the screen away from the History pop-up menu.

- If you have many items in your history for today, you get an Earlier Today item listed just above previous date items. Tap this to view all the web pages you visited today.

- If you tap the Bookmarks button at the top of the History pop-up menu, you can go up a level and see both Bookmarks and a menu item to take you back to your history.

Bookmarking Websites

While using Safari on the iPad, you need to bookmark some of the sites you visit most often. This can give you quick access to the information you need the most.

1. Use Safari to navigate to any web page.

2. Tap the Bookmarks/History button at the top of the screen.

3. Choose Add Bookmark.

4. Edit the title of the bookmark. The official title of the web page is prefilled, but you can use the keyboard to change it. You can tap the X to clear the text and start fresh.

Print It

You'll also notice the Print button when you tap the same button you use to create bookmarks. If you are using a printer compatible with Apple's AirPlay technology in your iPad, you can send the current page to a printer attached to your network. See "Printing from Your iPad" in Chapter 18 for details.

5. Tap the Bookmarks folder name to select a folder to place the bookmark.

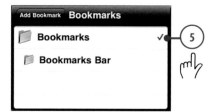

>>> Go Further

TIPS FOR BOOKMARKING WEBSITES

- You can save bookmarks to a folder called the Bookmarks Bar. These appear as buttons at the top of your browser. Only save the most important bookmarks to the Bookmarks Bar folder. These always show up at the top of your Safari screen.

- The titles of web pages are often long and descriptive. It is a good idea to shorten the title to something you can easily recognize, especially if it is a web page that you plan to visit often.

- You can create folders of bookmarks in your Bookmarks Bar folder. These appear as their own pop-up menu when you tap them, giving you direct access to a subset of your bookmarks.

Delete Your Bookmarks

Adding and using bookmarks is just the start. You eventually need to delete ones you don't use. You might find that over time you no longer need some bookmarks. Some might even link to missing or obsolete pages. There are two ways to delete a bookmark. The results of the two methods are the same; however, you might find the second method gives you a little more control.

Delete a Single Bookmark

The first method uses the Bookmarks list to locate and delete a single bookmark.

1. Tap the Bookmarks/History button at the top of the Safari screen. This brings up a list of bookmarks.

2. Swipe across a bookmark, from left to right, with your finger. This brings up a red Delete button.

3. Tap the Delete button to remove the bookmark. The bookmark is instantly deleted.

Another Way to Delete Bookmarks

This method for deleting bookmarks lets you unlock and delete bookmarks from the Bookmarks list.

1. Tap the Bookmarks/History button at the top of the Safari screen. This brings up a list of bookmarks.

2. Tap the Edit button at the upper-right corner. (It becomes the Done button.) Now each bookmark has a red circle with a line through it to its left.

3. Tap one of the red circles to unlock it. A Delete button appears to the right.

4. Tap the Delete button to remove the bookmark.

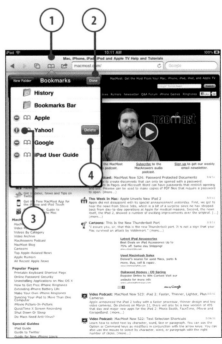

Sync Your Bookmarks

If you want to go to town and really organize your bookmarks, you might be better off doing so on your Mac or PC with the Safari browser. Syncing your iPad to your computer should sync your bookmarks as well. Safari on your computer gives you greater control over moving and deleting bookmarks. So just do your wholesale editing on your computer and resync.

Creating Home Screen Bookmarks

If a web page is somewhat important, you might want to create a bookmark for it. If it is extremely important and you need to go to it often, you might want to make sure that bookmark is saved to your Bookmarks Bar so that it is easily accessible.

However, if a web page is even more important to you than that, you can save it as an icon on your iPad's Home screen.

1. Use Safari to navigate to any web page.

2. Tap this button at the top of the screen.

3. Choose Add to Home Screen.

Managing Home Screen Bookmarks

You can arrange and delete Home screen bookmarks just like icons that represent apps. See "Arranging Apps on Your iPad" in Chapter 15 for details.

4. You can now edit the name of the page. Most web page titles are too long to display under an icon on the Home screen of the iPad, so edit the name down to as short a title as possible.

5. You can tap Cancel to leave this interface without sending the bookmark to the Home screen.

6. Tap Add to complete adding the icon to the Home screen.

Website Icons

The icon for this type of bookmark can come from one of two sources. Web page owners can provide a special iPhone/iPad icon that would be used whenever someone tries to bookmark her page.

However, if no such icon has been provided, your iPad can take a screen shot of the web page and shrink it down to make an icon.

Filling in Web Forms

The Web isn't a one-way street. Often you need to interact with web pages, filling in forms or text fields. Doing this on the iPad is similar to doing it on a computer, but with notable differences.

The keyboard shares screen space with the web page, so when you tap on a field, you bring up the keyboard at the bottom of the screen.

Also pull-down menus behave differently. On the iPad you get a special menu showing you all the options.

1. Use Safari to navigate to a web page with a form. For demonstration purposes, try one of the pages at http://apple.com/feedback/.

2. To type in a text field, tap that field.

3. The keyboard appears at the bottom of the screen. Use it to type text into the field.

4. Tap the Go button when you finish.

5. To select a check box or radio button, tap it just as you would click on it on your computer using the mouse.

6. To select an item in a pull-down menu, tap the menu.

7. The special iPad pull-down menu reacts like any other iPad interface. You can tap an item to select it. You can touch and drag up and down to view more selections if the list is long.

8. A check mark appears next to the currently selected item. Tap that item or any other one to select it and dismiss the menu.

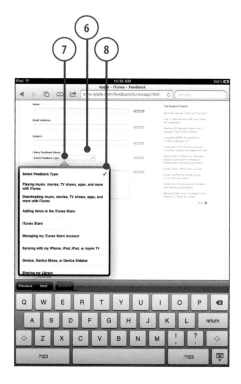

Special Menus

Some websites may use special menus that they build from scratch, rather than these default HTML menus. When this is the case, you get a menu that looks exactly like the one you get when viewing the web page on a computer. If the web page is well coded, it should work fine on the iPad, though it might be slightly more difficult to make a selection.

>> Go Further

TIPS FOR FILLING IN FORMS

- You can use the AutoFill button just above the keyboard to fill in your name, address, and other contact info instead of typing on the keyboard. To enable AutoFill, go into your iPad Settings and look for the AutoFill preferences under Safari. Also make sure your own information is correct and complete in your card in the Contacts application.

- To move between fields in a form, use the Previous and Next buttons just above the keyboard. You can quickly fill in an entire form this way without having to tap on the web page to select the next item.

Opening Multiple Web Pages

Safari on the iPad enables you to open multiple web pages at the same time. You can view only one at a time, but you can hold your place on a page while you look at something on another page.

1. While browsing the Web using Safari on the iPad, tap the Page button at the top of the screen.

2. You see your current page shrink to fill only one-ninth the size of the screen.

3. You can return to the current page by tapping it.

4. You can create a new page by tapping on the blank rectangle next to the current page. This returns you to the full screen view of Safari. Whatever you view on this new page does not affect what is still on the first page. You can browse and search on this new page.

5. Tap the Page button again and you see both your first and second pages displayed.

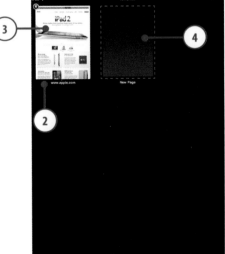

6. Tap either the first page or the second page to go to it. You can also tap the New Page rectangle to add yet another page. You can have up to nine active Web pages in Safari on the iPad.

TIPS FOR USING MULTIPLE WEB PAGES

>>> Go Further

- Another way to open up a second page is to tap and hold a link. Then you get a pop-up menu with the option to open the link in a new page.

- Using multiple pages is yet another way, besides bookmarks, to quickly access the same web page over and over again. Simply keep that page open when you finish viewing it and open a new page to browse elsewhere. Then tap the Page button to quickly return to the often-visited page.

Copying Text and Images from Web Pages

You can select text from web pages to copy and paste into your own documents or email messages.

1. Use Safari to navigate to a web page.

2. Tap and hold over a piece of text. You don't need to be exact because you can adjust the selection later. The word Copy appears above the selected area that is highlighted in light blue.

3. You can tap and drag one of the four blue dots to change the selection area. When your selection gets small enough, it changes to only two blue dots indicating the first and last character of the selection.

4. Tap outside the selection to cancel at any time.

5. Tap the Copy button over the selection to copy the text.

6. You can now go to another application such as Mail or Pages and tap in a text area to choose Paste and paste the text into the area. You can also do this in a form on a page in Safari, such as a web-based email form.

Using Images from Web Pages

Along with copying and pasting text from Safari, you can copy images and save them to your photo collection.

1. Use Safari to navigate to to a web page that has an image you want to save.

2. Tap and hold your finger on that image.

3. Select Save Image. This saves your image to your Saved Images folder in the Photos app. You can then use this image in any app where you select images from your photo albums.

4. Select Copy to copy the image to the Clipboard. You can then go to a program such as Mail or Pages and paste that image into the document you are composing.

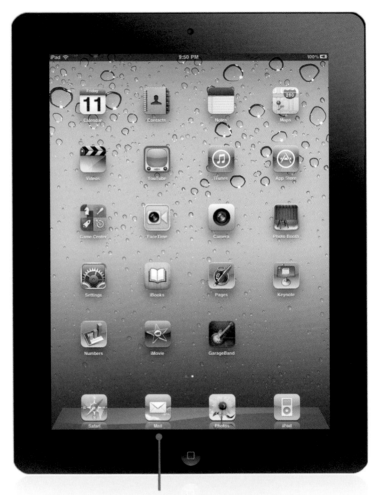

Send and receive email from your ISP
or a variety of popular email services.

Next we look at how to configure and use the Mail program on your iPad to correspond using email.

→ Configuring Your Email

→ Reading Your Email

→ Composing a New Message

→ Creating a Signature

→ Deleting and Moving Messages

→ Searching Email

→ Configuring How Email Is Received

→ More Email Settings

Communicating with Email

Now that you have a take-anywhere iPad with a battery that seems to last forever, you have no excuse for not replying to emails, so you need to be comfortable using the built-in Mail app that enables you to connect with your home or work email using standard protocols such as POP and IMAP. You can even connect with more proprietary systems such as AOL, Exchange, and Yahoo!.

Configuring Your Email

Here is a complete list of what information you need to set up your iPad for a traditional email account. If you have a service such as Exchange, Gmail, AOL, Yahoo!, or MobileMe, you won't need all this.

- Email Address

- Account Type (POP or IMAP)

- Incoming Mail Server Address

- Incoming Mail User ID

- Incoming Mail Password

- Outgoing Mail Server Address

- Outgoing Mail User ID

- Outgoing Mail Password

>>> Go Further

IMAP VERSUS POP

POP (Post Office Protocol) fetches and removes email from a server. The server acts as a temporary holding place for email. It is difficult to use POP if you receive email using both your iPad and a computer. You need to either deal with some email going to one device and some to another or set up one device to not remove email from the server so that the other device can retrieve it as well.

IMAP (Internet Message Access Protocol) makes the server the place where all messages are stored, and your iPad and computer simply display what is on the server. It is more ideal in situations where you have multiple devices getting email from the same account.

If you wonder why you shouldn't skip all the setup and just use webmail on your iPad, it's because you can't use emailing features in other apps—such as emailing web page links or emailing photos—if you don't configure the email settings.

1. Tap the Settings icon on your Home screen.

2. Tap Mail, Contacts, Calendars.

3. Tap Add Account.

4. If you have a Microsoft Exchange, MobileMe, Gmail, Yahoo! Mail, or AOL account, tap the corresponding button. From there, simply enter your information, and your iPad figures out the rest.

5. Tap Other if you have a traditional POP or IMAP account from work, your Internet providers, or a traditional hosting company.

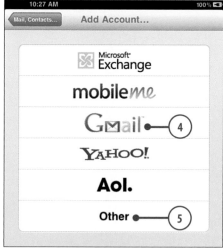

6. Tap Add Mail Account.

7. Tap in the Name field and enter your name.

8. Tap in the Address field and enter your email address.

9. Tap in the Password field and enter your password.

10. The Description field should automatically fill with a copy of your email address. Keep it or use another description for the account.

11. Tap Save.

12. Tap IMAP or POP as the email account type.

13. Tap in the Incoming Mail Server, Host Name field and enter your email host's address.

14. Tap in the Incoming Mail Server, User Name field and enter your user name.

15. Tap in the Incoming Mail Server, Password field and enter your password.

16. Repeat the previous three steps for Outgoing Mail Server.

17. Tap Save, and the verification process, which can take up to a minute, begins.

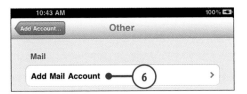

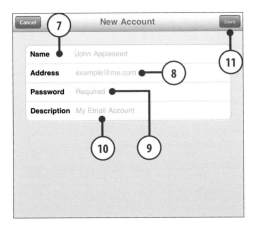

What if the Settings Won't Verify?

If your settings fail to verify, you need to double-check all the information you entered. When something is wrong, it often comes down to a single character being mistyped in one of these fields.

Reading Your Email

You use the Mail app to read your email, which is much easier to navigate and type in horizontal mode. Let's start by reading some email.

1. Tap the Mail app icon on the Home screen.

2. On the left you see a list of incoming mail. On the right, you see the selected message.

3. Tap a message to view it.

4. Tap the Refresh button to look for new mail.

5. Tap the Details button to see more fields, such as To: and Cc: email addresses.

6. Tap the email address of the sender.

7. Tap Create New Contact to add the sender to your contacts.

8. Tap Add to Existing Contact to add the email address to a contact you already have in your Contacts app.

9. Tap the Folder button at the top of the message.

10. Tap a folder to move the current message to that folder.

11. Tap the Trash button at the top of the message to send the message directly to the Trash folder.

12. Tap the arrow button at the top of the message to reply or forward the message.

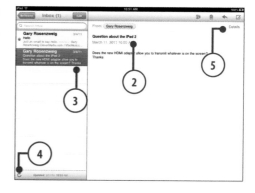

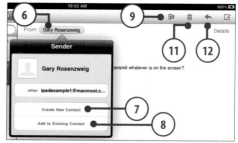

Multiple Inboxes

If you have more than one email account, you can choose to look at each inbox individually or a single unified inbox that includes messages from all accounts. Just tap the Mailboxes button at the upper-left corner of the screen and choose All Inboxes. You can also choose to look at the inbox of a single account, or dig down into any folder of an account.

How Do You Create Folders?

You can't create folders inside your mailbox on your iPad. If you use an IMAP mail server, you can go to the web interface for that server and create a new folder there so that it appears on your iPad. Sometimes you can even create folders for IMAP servers in Apple Mail or Windows Mail on your Mac or PC. Unfortunately, if you use a POP email server, you cannot indicate to the Mail app that you want more folders. You are stuck with Inbox, Sent, and Trash.

Composing a New Message

Whether you compose a new message or reply to one you received, the process is similar. Let's take a look at composing one from scratch.

1. In the Mail app, tap the Compose button.

2. Enter a To: address.

3. Alternatively, tap the + button to bring up a list of contacts, and choose from there.

4. Tap in the subject field and type a subject for the email.

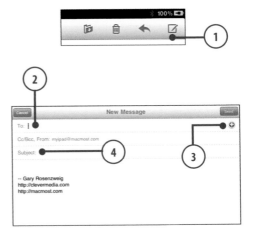

5. Tap below the subject field in the body of the email, and type your message.

6. Tap the Send button.

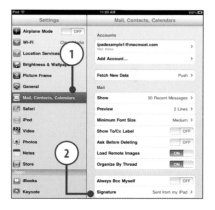

Including Images

You can copy and paste inside a Mail message just like you can inside of any text entry area on your iPad. But you can also paste in images! Just copy an image from any source—Photos app, Safari, and so on. Then tap in the message body and select Paste. You can paste in more than one image as well.

Creating a Signature

You can create a signature that appears below your messages automatically. You do this in the Settings app.

1. In the Settings app, choose Mail, Contacts, Calendars.

2. Tap Signature, which is way down in the list on the right.

3. Type a signature in the text field. You don't need to do anything to save the signature. You can tap the Home button on your iPad to exit Settings if you like.

Case-By-Case Signatures

You can have only one signature, even if you have multiple email accounts on your iPad. But the signature is placed in the editable area of the message composition field, so you can edit it like the rest of your message.

Deleting and Moving Messages

While viewing a message you can simply tap the Trash Can icon and move it to the trash. You can also move a group of messages to a folder or the trash.

1. In the Mail app, go to any mailbox and any subfolder, such as your Inbox.

2. Tap the Edit button.

3. Tap the circles next to each message to select them. They will be added to the middle of the screen in a slightly messy stack.

4. Tap the Delete button to delete the selected messages.

5. Tap the Move button, and the left side of the screen changes to a list of folders. You can select one to move all the messages to that folder.

6. Tap the Cancel button to exit without deleting or moving any messages.

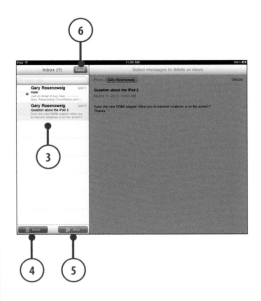

What About Spam?

Your iPad has no built-in spam filter. Fortunately, most email servers filter out spam at the server level. Using a raw POP or IMAP account from an ISP might mean you don't have any server-side spam filtering, unfortunately. But using an account at a service such as Gmail means that you get spam filtering on the server and junk mail automatically goes to the Junk folder, not your Inbox.

Searching Email

You can also search your messages using the Mail app.

1. In the Mail app, from a mailbox view, tap the Search field.

2. Type a search term.

3. Select From, To, Subject, or All to decide which part of the messages to search.

4. Select a message to view from the search results.

5. Tap the keyboard hide key at the bottom right to hide the keyboard.

6. Tap Cancel to exit the search and return to the mailbox you were previously viewing.

You Can't Search Messages

Searches work only on From, To, and Subject fields. You can't search the body of your messages. Even the All selection just searches the three fields and not the rest of the messages.

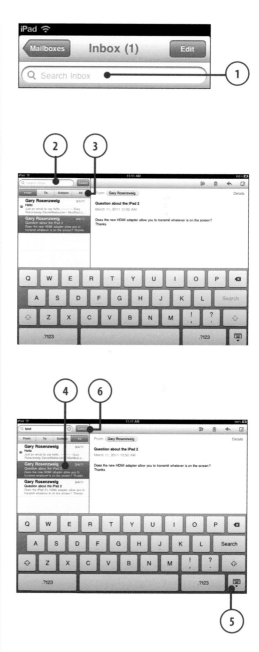

Configuring How Email Is Received

You have more settings for email beyond the basic account setup. You can decide how you want to receive email, using either push delivery (MobileMe and Microsoft Exchange) or fetch delivery (all other email accounts).

1. Go to the Settings app and tap on Mail, Contacts, and Calendars.

2. Tap Fetch New Data.

3. Turn on Push to use push email reception if you use email accounts that can send email via push.

4. Otherwise, select how often you want your iPad to go out to the server and fetch email.

5. Tap Advanced.

6. For each account using fetch, tap the account to turn Fetch to Fetch or Manual.

Push Settings

The two choices for most email accounts are Fetch and Manual. If you have a push account, such as MobileMe, you have three choices: Push, Fetch and Manual. You can switch a Push account to Fetch or Manual if you prefer.

More Email Settings

You can change even more email settings in the Settings app. Let's take a look at some of them.

1. Tap Show to choose the number of messages to show in your Inbox. You can choose 25, 50, 75, 100, or 200.

2. Tap Preview to choose how many lines of message preview to show when stacking messages up in the list view.

3. Tap Minimum Font Size to modify the size of the text in messages.

4. Turn Show To/Cc Label on to view "To" or "Cc" in each email listed so that you know if you were the primary recipient or someone who was just copied on an email to someone else.

5. Turn Ask Before Deleting on to require a confirmation when you tap the trash can button in Mail.

6. Turn Load Remote Images off so that images referenced in an mail but stored on a remote server are not shown in the message body.

7. To group replies to a message under the original message, select Organize By Thread. This is handy when you subscribe to email discussion lists.

8. Turn Always Bcc Myself on if you want to get a copy of every email you send so that later you can move your copies of emails to your Sent folder on your computer.

9. Tap Default Account to determine which account is used to send email by default if you have more than one account set up on your iPad.

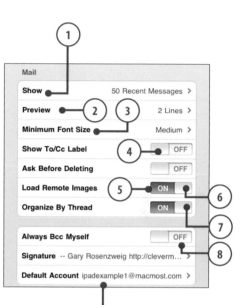

10. In most apps from which you send emails, you can type a message and also change the account you use to send the email.

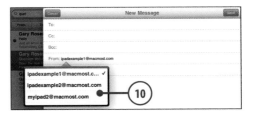

Why Not Show Remote Images?

The main reason to not show remote images is bandwidth. If you get an email that has 15 images referenced in it, you need to download a lot of data, and it takes a while for that email to show up completely. However, remote images are often used as ways to indicate whether you have opened and looked at messages. So turning this off might break some statistics and receipt functionality expected from the sender.

Take
pictures
with the
iPad's
cameras.

Browse your photos on
the iPad's brilliant screen.

In this chapter, we use the Photos app to view your pictures and create slideshows.

→ Taking Photos

→ Using Photo Booth

→ Browsing Your Photos

→ Using the Photos App

→ Viewing Albums

→ Creating a Slideshow

→ Turning Your iPad into a Picture Frame

→ Capturing the Screen

→ Deleting Photos

9

Taking and Viewing Photos

In addition to replacing books, the iPad replaces photo albums. You can literally carry thousands of photos with you on your iPad. Plus, your iPad's screen is a beautiful way to display these photos.

To access photos on your iPad, you first must sync them from your computer. Then you can use the Photos app to browse and view your photos.

With the iPad 2's cameras, you can also take photos with your iPad. You can view those in the Photos app as well.

Taking Photos

The iPad 2 has two cameras that you can use to take photos. The primary app for doing this is the Camera app.

1. Launch the Camera app from the home page. This brings up the Camera app, and you should immediately see the image from one of the two cameras.

2. First, locate the switch at the bottom-right corner of the screen. Make sure it's switched to camera (left) instead of video (right).

3. Tap the button at the upper right to switch between front and rear cameras.

4. Tap anywhere on the image to specify that you want to use that portion of the image to determine the exposure for the photo.

5. After you have tapped on the image, and if you are using the rear-facing camera, you will see a zoom slider at the bottom of the screen.

6. Tap the large camera button at the center of the screen along the bottom to take the picture.

7. Tap the button at the lower left to go to Camera Roll and see the pictures you have taken.

8. Tap the middle of the image to bring up controls on the top and bottom of the screen.

9. Use the slider at the bottom to flip through images you have taken that are in your Camera Roll.

10. Tap Camera Roll to exit viewing this one image and jump to an icon view of all of your Camera Roll photos.

11. Tap to start a slideshow of Camera Roll pictures.

12. Tap to email, Print, or Copy the photo.

13. Tap to send the photo to an Apple TV or other device using AirPlay.

14. Tap to delete the Photo.

15. Tap Done to return to the Camera app to take another photo.

It's Not All Good

THE iPAD IS A POOR PHOTO CAMERA

The resolution of the iPad's cameras is pretty low tech when it comes to taking still images. You only get a 960x720 image from the rear camera and a 640x480 image from the front. These are fine for video, but are merely toys when it comes to photography. You are better off using your mobile phone's camera in most cases. But for posting quick pictures to the Internet, it works fine.

Using Photo Booth

In addition to the basic picture-taking functionality of the Camera app, you can also use the included Photo Booth app to take more creative shots using one of eight special filters.

1. Launch the Photo Booth app.

2. You'll start by seeing all the filters you can choose from. Tap one of the filters to select it.

3. Now you'll see just that one filter. In addition, you have some buttons. Tap on the button at the bottom right to switch between the front and rear cameras.

4. Tap the button at the bottom left to return to the 9-filter preview.

5. Tap the camera button at the bottom to take a picture.

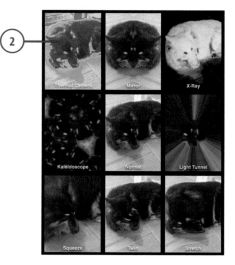

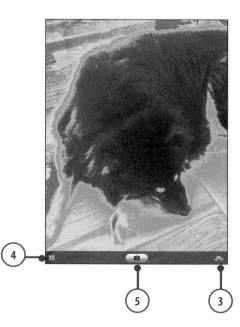

6. Some filters also allow you to tap the live video image to adjust the filter. For instance, the Light Tunnel filter enables you to set the position of the center of the tunnel.

7. As you take photos, they drop down to the bottom of the screen in a list. Select one and you'll get an X button to delete it.

8. Tap the button at the lower right to select photos to copy or email. All the pictures are placed in your Camera Roll as you take them, so you can also access them from the Photos app.

A Kind of Flash

When you take a picture with the camera on the front of the iPad, you get a kind of flash effect from the screen. It simply turns all white for a second. This helps in low light situations.

6

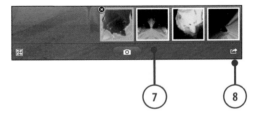

7   8

TWO DISTINCT TYPES OF PHOTOS

The key to understanding the Photos app is to realize that there are two distinct types of photos on your iPad. There are photos you have created on your iPad using either the built-in cameras, the screen capture functionality, or a third-party app that creates an image. These are all called Saved Photos. They were created on your iPad, so they appear as part of your Saved Photos album, also called the Camera Roll.

The second type of photo is one that has been synced from your computer. These photos appear arranged in albums that come from your iPhoto or PC pictures collections.

You can't mix these types of photos in albums. In fact, you can't arrange photos into albums at all. That's something you would do on your computer. So if you take a bunch of pictures with your iPad's camera, and you want to put them into albums, the way to do it is to sync with your computer, transferring the pictures there. Next, arrange the pictures into albums, and then sync back to your iPad.

Think of your iPad as you would any other digital camera. You take pictures and then sync to your computer. The fact that the iPad is also a great photo viewer is a separate function altogether. It gets confusing because as you will see next, you use the same app to browser both kinds of photos.

Browsing Your Photos

After you have synced to your Mac or PC, you should have some photos on your iPad, provided you have set some to sync in either iPhoto or iTunes. Then you can browse them with the Photos app.

1. Tap on the Photos app icon to launch it.

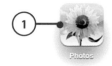

2. Tap one of the viewing options. You should have two to five choices, depending on how you synced your iPad.

3. Tap Photos to make sure you are in photo viewing mode.

4. Drag and scroll vertically or flick vertically to move through all the photos on your iPad.

5. Tap a photo to view that one. For most photos, you might want to rotate the iPad to its horizontal orientation for wide-screen viewing.

You Can't Edit, Not Even a Little Bit

The Photos app is strictly a viewer. You can't edit photos or make adjustments like you can in iPhoto. You can't even move photos from one album to another. All editing and organization must be done on your Mac or PC before you sync. However, there are many third-party apps that allow you to import a photo from your albums, edit them, and then export a new copy of the photo back to your Camera Roll. One example is the free Adobe Photoshop Express app.

6. To move to the next or previous photo, drag left or right.

7. To bring up controls at the top and bottom of a photo, tap in the center of the screen.

8. You can tap and run your finger over the small thumbnails at the bottom of the screen to move through photos.

9. Tap the All Photos button at the top of the screen to return to the list of photos.

ZOOM AND ROTATE

Here are a few tips on how to navigate your photos as you view them:

- Touch two fingers to the screen while viewing a photo, and pinch or unpinch to zoom out and in.

- Double-tap a photo to zoom back out to normal size.

- While a photo is at normal size, double-tap to zoom it to make it fit on the screen with the edges cropped.

- If you pinch in far enough, the picture closes, and you return to the browsing mode.

Using the Photos App

Although you can't edit a photo, you can use one for a few things on your iPad.

1. Tap the boxed arrow button in the upper-right corner.

2. Tap Email Photo from the list.

3. After you tap Email Photo, the Mail app launches and starts a new message. The photo is attached to the message.

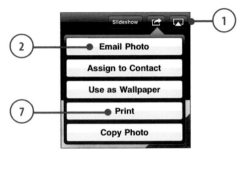

It's Not the Original Image

If you sync a photo from your computer to your iPad, and then email it to people, they actually receive a reduced image, not the original. iPad albums contain reduced images to save space. If you want to send the original, email it from your computer.

4. Tap Assign to Contact to display a list of all your contacts so that you can add the photo to the contact's thumbnail image.

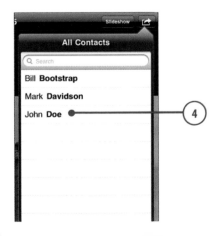

5. Tap Use as Wallpaper to assign the image to either the Lock Screen background or the Home screen background, or both.

6. Tap Copy Photo to copy the photo to the clipboard. To copy more than one image, tap the boxed arrow button while viewing your photos, and then select one or more photos to email or copy.

7. Tap Print to send to a printer on your network. See "Printing from Your iPad" in Chapter 18.

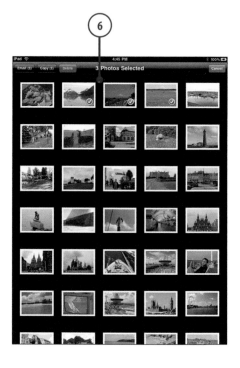

Viewing Albums

Looking at a huge list of photos is not the best way to view your collection. Using Albums is the simplest way to organize them.

1. In the Photos app, tap the Albums button. Most of the albums will correspond to your iPhoto albums or your folders if you sync images from your computer's file system.

2. Tap on an album to expand it to see all the photos.

3. Tap any photo to view it.

4. Tap the Albums button to return to the list of albums.

Getting Back to the Album

After you finish digging down into an album, you can go back to the list of albums by pressing the Albums button, or a similarly named button, at the top left. But you can also pinch in all photos to group them in the middle of the screen and then release to move back to the albums list.

5. Tap Places to see your geo-tagged photos (those marked with GPS locations).

6. Tap a pin on the map and a set of photos appears above it.

7. Tap the set of photos to dig down into the pictures.

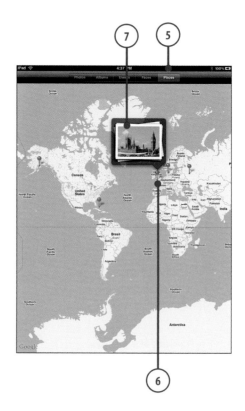

Creating a Slideshow

Another way to look at your photos is as a slideshow with music and transitions.

1. Tap on the Photos app icon to launch it.

2. Go to your Photos list, or select Album, Event, Faces, or Places.

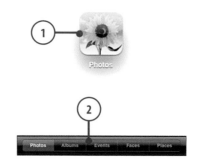

3. Tap the Slideshow button.

4. Switch the Play Music button on or off.

5. If you want to use music, tap to select a song from your iTunes collection.

6. Choose a transition.

7. Tap Start Slideshow.

Stopping a Slideshow

Tap on the screen anywhere to stop a slideshow.

Slideshow on TV

Want to present a slideshow on a monitor or TV? Use one of the video adapters discussed in Chapter 18 to hook your iPad up to a projector or a TV. Or, you can use AirPlay to stream the slideshow from your iPad to an Apple TV or other AirPlay device. Just tap on the slideshow while it is running and look for the AirPlay button at the upper-right corner. See "Using AirPlay To Play Music and Video on Other Devices" in Chapter 4.

Turning Your iPad into a Picture Frame

You can also set your iPad to show a slideshow when you are not in the Photos app. The Picture Frame function is configured in Settings, and then you activate it from the Lock screen.

1. Go to the Settings app.

2. Tap Picture Frame.

3. Choose either the Dissolve or Origami transition.

4. Turn Zoom in on Faces on or off. When it is on, pictures with faces in them are zoomed and cropped to show the faces close up.

5. Turn Shuffle on to show photos in random order.

6. Choose either All Photos, Albums, Faces, or Events.

7. Depending on your choice in step 6, you can check off one or more albums, faces, or events.

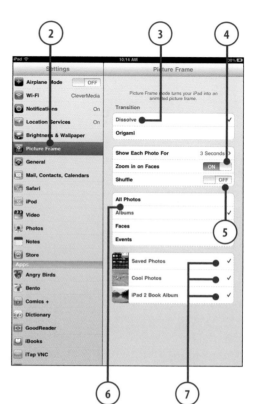

Picture Frame Album

If you want ultimate control over your picture frame slideshow and you use a Mac, create a special album in iPhoto called something like "iPad Picture Frame" and fill it with just the photos you want to use. Make sure you set iTunes to sync this photo album. Then set your Picture Frame settings to show only this one album.

8. Lock your iPad by pressing the Wake/Sleep button at the top of the device.

9. Press the Home button to bring up the Lock screen.

10. Without unlocking your iPad, tap the Picture Frame button to the right of the Slide to Unlock switch to put your iPad in Picture Frame mode.

11. Tap the screen at any time to bring back the Lock Screen controls so that you can unlock your iPad.

Capturing the Screen

You can capture the entire iPad screen and send it to your Photos app. This feature is useful if you want to save what you see to an image for later.

1. Make sure the screen shows what you want to capture. Try the Home screen, as an example.

2. Press and hold the Wake/Sleep button and Home button at the same time. The screen flashes and you hear a camera shutter sound, unless you have the volume turned down.

3. Go to the Photos app.

4. Tap on the Saved Photos album. The last image in this album should be your new screen capture. Tap it to open it.

5. The example is a vertical capture of the Home screen, so it might be confusing to look at. Turn your iPad horizontally.

6. Tap the boxed arrow icon to email the photo or copy it to use in another application. Or you can leave the photo in your Saved Photos album for future use.

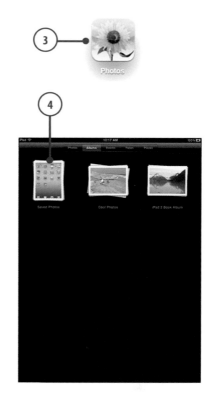

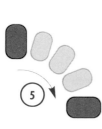

Deleting Photos

You can only delete photos from the Camera Roll album (some-times referred to as the "Saved Photos" album).

1. In Photos, go to the Albums view.

2. Tap on Camera Roll.

3. Tap a photo to view it.

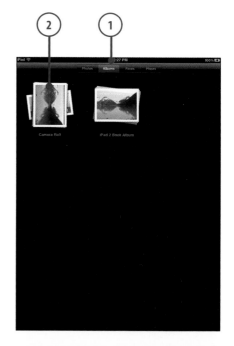

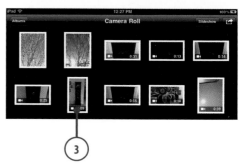

4. Tap the Trash Can button.

5. Tap Delete Photo.

6. Alternatively, you can go back to step 2 and then tap the boxed arrow button.

7. Tap multiple photos to select them.

8. Tap Delete.

So How Can I Delete Other Photos?

The Camera Roll album is special; it contains photos created on your iPad. The rest of the albums are just copies of photos synced from your computer. You can't delete them from your iPad any more than you can delete music synced to your iPad.

To delete these photos, go back to iPhoto on your computer, and remove them from any albums that you have set to sync to your iPad. Also, go into iTunes on your computer, and make sure the photo syncing options there—such as to sync Last 12 Months—won't copy that photo.

If you think of your photos like you think of your music, understanding which photos are synced and why makes more sense.

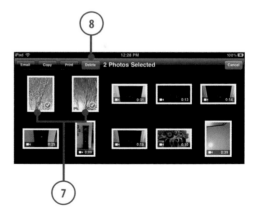

Make video calls
with FaceTime.

Record video with your
iPad's two cameras.

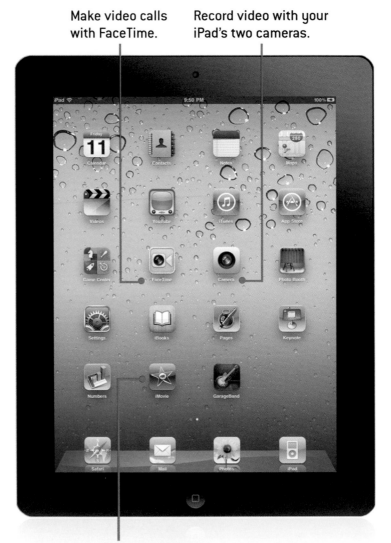

Put together movies from
your video clips and photos.

In this chapter, we use the Camera, Photo Booth, and iMovie apps to shoot and edit video with your iPad. We'll also use the FaceTime app to make a video call.

→ Shooting Video

→ Trimming Video Clips

→ Combining Clips in iMovie

→ Editing Transitions in iMovie

→ Adding Photos to Your Video in iMovie

→ Adding Video Titles in iMovie

→ Creating a FaceTime Account

→ Placing Video Calls with FaceTime

→ Receiving Video Calls with FaceTime

Recording Video

You can record video using either of the two cameras on your iPad 2. The primary app for doing this is the Camera app.

In addition, you can edit video with the iMovie app. This app, which you can purchase from Apple in the App Store, lets you combine clips and add transitions, titles, and audio.

The cameras on your iPad can also be used to video chat with someone on another iPad, an iPhone, iPod Touch, or a Mac using the FaceTime app.

Shooting Video

If you simply want to record something that is happening using the cameras, you can do it with the Camera app.

1. Launch the Camera app.

2. Switch the camera mode to video.

3. Toggle between the rear and front cameras.

4. Optionally, tap in the image to set the best point for the exposure setting.

5. Start recording. While you are recording, the red dot will flash and the length of the recording will show in the upper-right corner. Press the same button to stop recording.

6. Tap here to view your video when you are done.

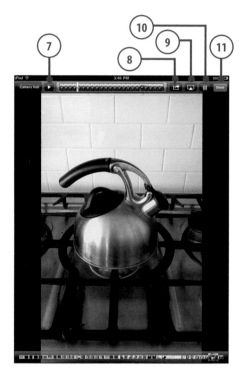

7. You are now in the Camera Roll, the same place as you were in "Taking Photos," in Chapter 9. But the interface looks different when you have a video instead of a still photo. Tap the play button to watch the video.

8. Tap here to email or copy the video, or send it to your YouTube account.

9. Tap the AirPlay button to stream the video over Apple TV or another AirPlay device.

10. Tap the trashcan to delete the video.

11. When you are done viewing your video, tap Done to shoot another.

It's Not All Good

EMAILING COMPRESSES THE VIDEO

Video with the rear camera is shot at 1280x720, high definition. But when you email a video, it is compressed to 272x480, a miniature version of your original. This is good because you won't be sending a massive video file, using your bandwidth and the bandwidth of the recipient. But don't use email to save your videos to your computer. Instead, sync and transfer, as you would do with photos.

Trimming Video Clips

While viewing a video in the Camera Roll, you can also trim it to cut some unneeded footage from the start and end of the video.

1. You can get to the Camera Roll by either using the Photos app or the Camera app. For instance, launch the Camera app and immediately tap the image in the lower left on the screen.

2. If you are viewing a video, you will see a timeline of sorts at the top of the screen.

3. Drag the left side of the timeline to the right to trim from the start of the video.

4. Drag the right side of the timeline to the right to trim from the end of the video.

5. Tap the Trim button.

6. Tap Trim Original to replace the video with the trimmed version.

7. Tap Save as New Clip to keep the original, and also save your trimmed version as a separate clip.

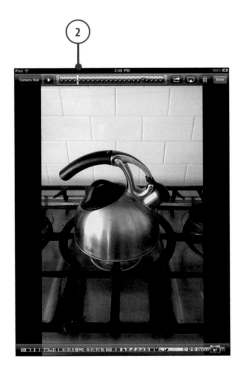

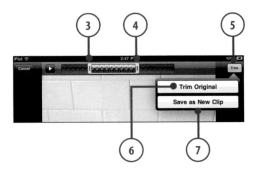

Combining Clips in iMovie

The trimming functionality of the Camera and Photos apps gives you the basic ability to edit a video clip, but you can go a lot further if you purchase the iMovie app from Apple. Although not a full-featured editor like you might have on your computer, you can combine clips, add titles and transitions, and produce a short video from your clips.

1. Launch the iMovie app. Turn your iPad to look at the screen horizontally. iMovie is a little easier to use in that orientation.

2. Tap the + button to create a new project.

3. You can add a video to your project by tapping on a clip on the left, and then tapping the blue down arrow to place it in the timeline at the bottom.

4. You can also record new video clips using the camera button at the right.

5. Continue to add more clips. Each one will be appended to the end of the project.

6. The red line indicates the current position of the video.

7. The preview area shows you the image at the current position.

8. You can drag the project timeline left and right to scroll through it.

9. You can pinch in and out to shrink or enlarge the timeline.

10. Press play to play the video in the preview area. If the red line is at the end of the video, it will jump back to the start of the video first.

11. Tap and hold a clip, and you can drag it to a different part of the project timeline.

12. Tap the My Projects button when you are done editing. There is no need to "save" your project—the current state of the project is always saved.

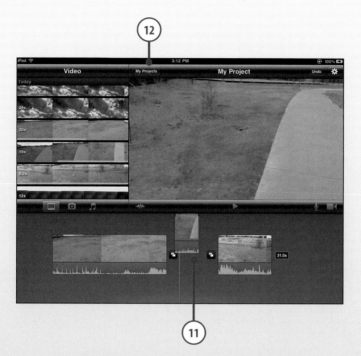

13. Tap the name of the project in the theater marquee to edit the name.

14. Tap the play button to view the finished project.

15. Tap the export button to send the video to your Camera Roll, export it to iTunes the next time you sync, or upload to one of the listed Internet video sites.

Best Way to Share with Friends?

While it may seem to be a good idea to simply email a video to your friends, remember that video files are usually very large. Even if you have the bandwidth to upload them, your friends need the bandwidth to download them. Some may have restrictions on how large email attachments can be.

So, the video sharing options in iMovie are better for all concerned. You can upload to your Facebook or YouTube account and even set the video to "private" or "unlisted." Then just let a few friends know about it with the link in an email instead of a huge file attachment.

Editing Transitions in iMovie

Between each clip in your iMovie project is a transition. You can choose between a direct cut (no transition), a cross dissolve transition, or a special theme transition. But first, you must select a theme.

1. Open up the project you created in the previous example.

2. Tap the settings button at the upper right to select a theme.

3. Flip through the themes and choose one.

4. Double-tap one of the transition buttons that appear between each clip. This should bring up the Transition Settings menu.

5. Choose None if you want one clip to start right after the other.

6. Choose Cross Dissolve if you want one clip to fade into the other.

7. Choose Theme to use the special theme transition. These vary depending on which theme you choose.

8. Choose a duration for the transition.

9. Tap the triangles below the transition button to expand into a precision editor.

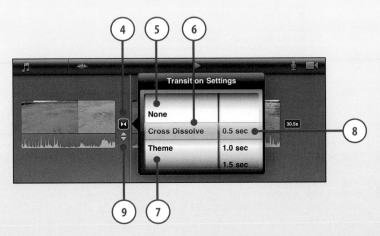

10. Move the transition area to select how you want the two clips to overlap during the transition.

11. Tap the triangles to leave the precision edit mode.

Transition Previews?

Unfortunately, you can't really preview the transitions in iMovie for iPad. You just have to apply a theme and then see what the transitions look like. Plus, the theme applies to the entire project, so you can't mix and match transitions. iMovie for iPad doesn't give you much control over the details. It is more for people who want to create a quick, nice-looking video without playing around with the details.

Adding Photos to Your Video in iMovie

You can also add photos from your Camera Roll or any album on your iPad. You can just use a series of photos in a video, or mix photos and video clips.

1. Continuing with the previous example, scroll the timeline all the way to the left.

2. Tap the photos button.

3. Tap the name of the album that contains your photo.

4. Tap the photo you want to use.

5. It now appears in the timeline at the current position. Tap it to select it.

Pictures in Projects

Pictures in iMovie projects don't just sit there; they move. For instance, the picture may start out fitting in the screen, and then slowly zoom in on a specific spot. Or, it may start showing the upper left and pan down to the lower right. You can control where the movement starts and ends.

>>> Go Further

GETTING CREATIVE WITH PICTURES

You can even create a video without any photos. For example, you could use one of the drawing programs mentioned in Chapter 16, such as SketchBook Pro, Brushes, ArtStudio, or Adobe Ideas, to create images with text and drawings on them. Create a series to illustrate an idea or story. Then bring them together as a series of pictures in an iMovie project. Add music and a voice over to make something very interesting.

6. Tap and drag the yellow dots to change the duration of the photo in the timeline. It starts with a default of 5 seconds. But, for example, you could increase it to 10 seconds.

7. Tap the Start button that appears in the preview area. Then adjust the photo by pinching zooming and dragging to get it just as you like. For instance, pinch in so the photo fits into the frame.

8. Tap the End button at the upper right to set the end position for the picture. For instance, unpinch to zoom in on a specific area.

9. Tap Done when you finish adjusting both the start and end positions.

10. Slide the timeline back and forth to preview how the movement in the picture will work.

    You can continue to add pictures just as you would add video clips. Add as many as you like. You can even create a slideshow of just photos without ever shooting a single second of video footage.

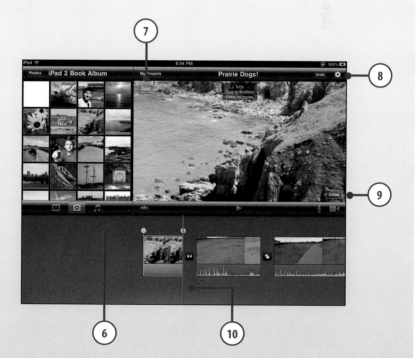

Adding Video Titles in iMovie

You can also add titles that overlay clips or photos in iMovie. Like the transitions, the style of the titles depends on the theme you are using.

1. Continue with the example we have been building. Double-tap on a clip to select it and bring up the Clip Settings menu.

2. Tap Title Style.

3. Select a title style. As you do so, a preview appears in the preview area.

4. Tap in the text field area in the preview to bring up the keyboard, and enter text.

5. Some title types show a map or have a space where the location is displayed. Tap Location to enter a name for the location.

MUSIC AND VOICEOVERS

You can also do a lot with the audio in iMovie. You can add any song from your iPad's iTunes collection to the video as the background track. There are also a number of theme music tracks included that you can use.

You can also add from a collection of sound effects the same way. However, sound effects can appear at any point in your movie, whereas music covers the entire span of the video.

You can also record a voiceover so you can narrate your video. This means you can have four audio tracks: the audio attached to the video, background music, sound effects, and a voiceover.

To learn how to use all the additional features of iMovie, look for the help button at the bottom-left corner of the projects screen. This brings up complete documentation for the app.

Creating a FaceTime Account

Another major use of the video cameras is FaceTime. This is Apple's video calling service. You can make video phone calls between any devices that have FaceTime. At the present time, this includes the iPhone 4, the most recent iPod touch, Macs, and the iPad 2. As the number of people with FaceTime increases, this will become more useful.

All that is required to make a FaceTime call is a free account. You can use your existing Apple ID or create a new one right in the FaceTime app.

1. Launch the FaceTime app.

2. On the initial screen, select Create New Account.

3. Fill in all the fields. You can use any email address—it doesn't have to be a MobileMe one.

4. Tap Next.

5. Even after you have created your account using an email address, you can still choose another email address to use as your FaceTime address. This is like your phone number. It is what people will use to place a FaceTime call to you.

6. Tap Next.

Now that you have a FaceTime account, you can place and receive calls. But remember you still need to be connected to the Internet with a Wi-Fi connection. At this time, mobile carriers do not support FaceTime over their 3G networks.

Placing Video Calls with FaceTime

After you have your account set up in FaceTime, you can place and receive calls.

1. Launch the FaceTime app.

2. Select a contact from your list. If your contact list isn't showing, tap the Contacts button at the bottom right of the screen.

3. Alternatively, you can add a new contact. You need to know either their iPhone 4 phone number or the email address they used when creating their FaceTime account.

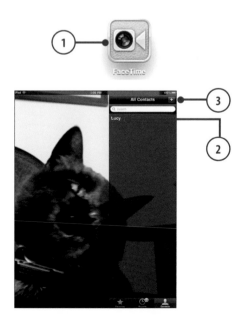

4. Tap the phone number or email address for the contact to initiate a FaceTime call.

5. Wait while the call is placed. You'll hear a ringing. You can tap the End button to cancel the call.

6. After the other party has answered the call, you can see both her image filling the whole screen and your image in the upper right. You can drag your image to any of the four corners.

7. Tap the mute button to mute your microphone.

8. Tap the switch cameras button to show the view from the rear camera.

9. Tap End to finish the call.

Two-Way Street

In order for you to place a FaceTime call, of course, the recipient also needs to have FaceTime set up. You can tell in step 4 that this has been done because of the blue camera icon next to the phone number. Otherwise, if she has a FaceTime-compatible device, you need to get her to set up an account before trying to initiate a FaceTime connection.

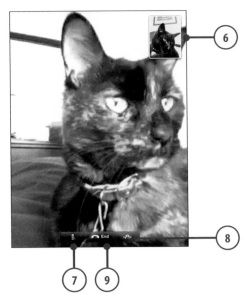

Receiving Video Calls with FaceTime

After you have a FaceTime account, you can receive calls as well. Here's how to check to make sure you can get calls, and what happens when you receive one.

1. Launch the Settings app.

2. Tap on FaceTime on the left.

3. You can turn off FaceTime, preventing you from getting any calls.

4. You can view and change your account.

5. You can change or add more email addresses that can be used by people trying to reach you via FaceTime.

Dead Ringer

So what happens when you get a call? It depends on what you are doing at the time. If your iPad is asleep, a version of the lock screen will appear.

6. You'll see something similar to the lock screen, but with a live feed from your camera (so you can see if you look good enough to video chat) and the caller's name at the top.

7. Slide the Slide to Answer button to the right to wake up your iPad and go immediately into the call.

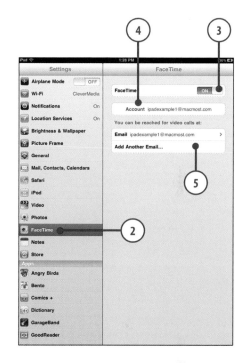

8. If you are using your iPad at the time the call comes in, FaceTime launches and you get a screen with two buttons. The screen will still show your camera's image and the name of the caller.

9. Tap Decline to ignore the call.

10. Tap Accept to start the video call.

Ring Ring

Remember that you can set your ringtone in the Settings app under Sounds. You can even set the volume for rings to be unaffected by the volume controls on the side of your iPad. That way you don't miss a call because you left the volume turned down.

>>> Go Further

SO WHAT IF IT DOESN'T WORK?

FaceTime is set up to be simple. It just works. Except when it doesn't. There are no network settings to fiddle with. So the problem usually lies in the wi-fi router at either end of the call. If someone has security on their modem or Wi-Fi router, then it could be interfering with the call. See this document at Apple's site for some FaceTime troubleshooting tips: http://support.apple.com/kb/ht4319.

Write and
design
complex
documents.

In this chapter, we begin to get work done on the iPad by using Pages to create and format documents.

11

→ Creating a New Document

→ Styling Text

→ Reusing Styles

→ Formatting Text

→ Creating Lists

→ Column Layouts

→ Inserting Images

→ Using Shapes in Documents

→ Creating Tables

→ Creating Charts

→ Document Setup

→ Transferring Documents to and from Pages with iTunes

Writing with Pages

So far we've mostly been looking at ways to consume media—music, video, books, photos, and so on. The next three chapters deal with the iWork suite of applications: Pages, Numbers, and Keynote.

We start with Pages, the word processor, which you can use for a fair amount of layout and design. Pages is not one of the iPad's built-in apps. You need to purchase and download it from the Apps Store.

Creating a New Document

Let's start off simple. The most basic use of Pages is to create a new document and enter some text.

1. Tap the Pages app icon on the Home screen. Most likely, the Pages app is located on the second page of your Home screen. You should start in the My Documents list. If not, tap the My Documents button at the upper-left corner to go there.

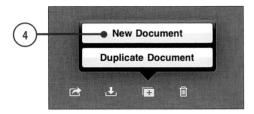

2. The sample document that teaches you a little bit about Pages displays. Tap it and scroll vertically through it if you like.

3. Otherwise, tap the + button at the bottom of the screen to start a new document.

4. Tap New Document.

5. The template choices display. You can scroll vertically to see more. Tap the Blank template to go into the main editing view.

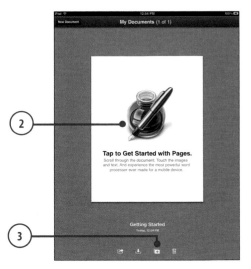

A Different Angle

When you turn your iPad on its side, the horizontal view of the editing screen is very different. There are no toolbars or buttons. There's just a keyboard and the page with your text. If you want to apply styling and formatting, make sure you're in vertical mode.

6. Type some sample text in the document just to get the feel for entering text.

7. Return to your documents list by tapping My Documents.

8. Browse through your documents by swiping left and right. You should have two documents now, the one you just created and the sample document.

9. With the document you want to edit in the center of the screen, tap it to open that document.

10. With the document you want to delete in the center of the screen, tap the Trash icon to delete it.

A Real Keyboard

If you plan on using Pages on your iPad often, you might want to invest in a physical keyboard for your iPad. You can use the Apple Wireless keyboard or almost any Bluetooth keyboard. Apple also has a version of the iPad dock that includes a keyboard. See Chapter 18, "iPad Accessories," for details.

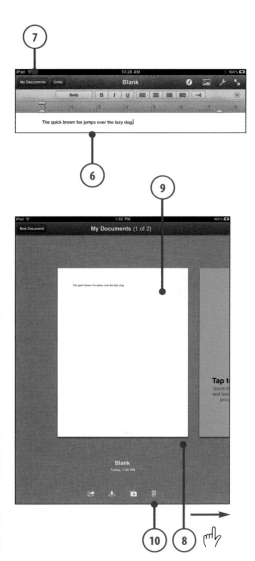

Styling Text

Now let's learn how to style text. You can change the font, style, and size.

1. In an open document, double-tap a word to select it.

2. Pull on the blue dots to select the area you want to style.

3. Use the toolbar buttons to format your text as bold, italic, or underline.

Undo Mistakes

At the top of the Pages screen, there is an Undo button. Use that to undo the last action you took—whether it is typing some text or changing styles. You can use Undo multiple times to go back several steps.

---

4. Tap the i button to bring up the Style/List/Layout menu.

5. Tap Style.

6. Tap the B, *I*, and U buttons to format text. Tap the buttons a second time if you want to change the style back to plain text. The fourth button, S, styles the text as strikethrough.

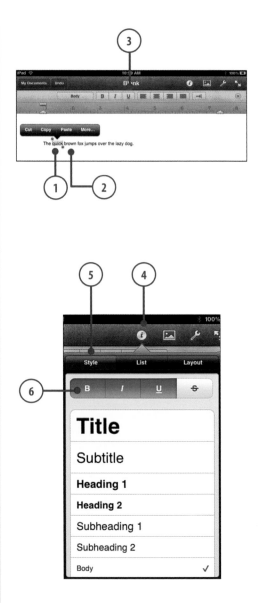

7. Under the text formatting buttons are some preset styles you can use. Drag the list up to reveal Text Options and tap it.

8. Set the font size, color, and type. Tap on the top and bottom halves of the font size indicator to increase and decrease the font size.

9. Tap the Color button to get a selection of colors.

10. Tap a color or drag to the left to look at grayscale options.

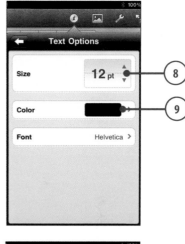

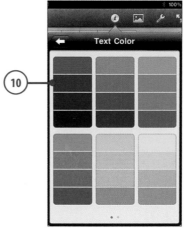

11. The black color tile has a check mark in it to indicate that it is the current color of the text. Swipe back and choose a different color, such as red.

12. Tap the left-facing arrow above the colors to return to the Text Options menu.

13. Tap Font.

14. Drag in the list of fonts to view them all.

15. Tap a font to change the selected text to it.

16. Tap the blue button to the right of most fonts to view font variations.

17. Tap outside of the menu to dismiss it and return to editing.

Printing Pages

You can print a document from Pages, Numbers, or Keynote if you have one of the printers compatible with Apple's AirPrint technology built into your iPad. Tap the tool button (it looks like a wrench in the upper-right corner) and then tap Print. You'll be prompted to select a printer, page range, and number of copies. See "Printing from Your iPad" in Chapter 18.

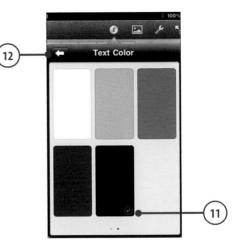

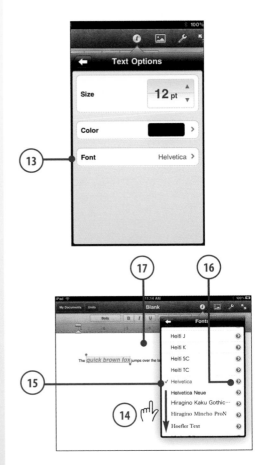

Reusing Styles

So what if you define the font, style, and size for something in Pages, and you want to use it again with another section of text? Just copy and paste the style from one piece of text to others.

1. Select some text.

2. If you already have a style in the clipboard, you see a More option; tap it. Otherwise, you might see the Copy Style option appear without needing to tap More.

3. Tap Copy Style.

4. Select another piece of text.

5. Tap More (as shown in step 2) and then tap Paste Style.

6. Your style is copied to the selected text.

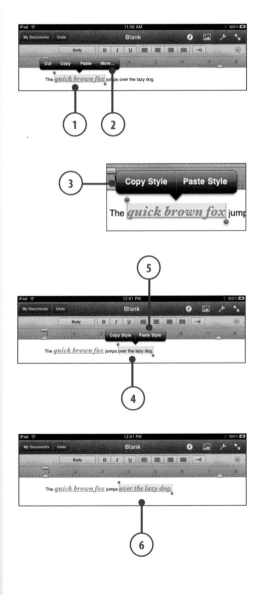

Formatting Text

The next step is to learn how to format and align text, which you do mostly through the toolbars at the top of the Pages screen in vertical mode.

1. Continue to work with the sample document, or start a new one and add some text.

2. Tap in the text so that the cursor is somewhere in the line. It can be at the beginning, the middle, or the end, so long as it is not on another line.

3. Tap the center alignment button in the toolbar to center the text. You can use the left, right, or justified buttons in the same set to align the text differently.

4. Tap at the end of the line to place the cursor there.

5. Tap the return key on the onscreen keyboard to go to the next line.

6. Tap the left alignment button in the toolbar.

7. Type some sample text, just a word or two.

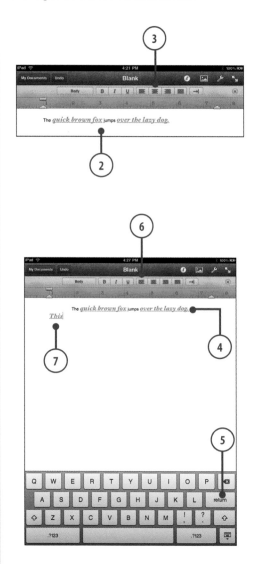

8. Tap the button in the toolbar to see choices for tabs and breaks.

9. Tap Tab on the drop-down menu to insert a tab.

10. Type another sample word. Because the new line of text inherited the underline format of the previous line, we can clearly see the extra space inserted between the words by the tab. We haven't added any tab stops to the document yet, so the position just defaults to the next inch.

11. Tap in the ruler around the 3-inch marker to insert a tab stop and move the second word over to match this tab stop's horizontal position.

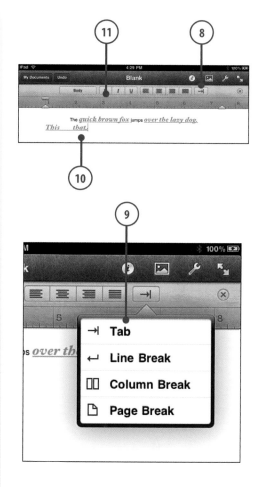

More Tab Options

If you like tabs, you'll be happy to know you can make centered tabs, right tabs, and dotted tabs as you would on a desktop word processor. Just double-tap a tab in the ruler, and it changes to the next type. To remove a tab, just tap and drag it down and out of the ruler.

Creating Lists

You can easily create lists in Pages, just like in a normal word processor.

1. Create a new document in Pages using the Blank template.

2. Type a word that could be the first item in a list. Don't tap return.

3. Tap the i button on the toolbar.

4. Tap List.

5. Tap the Bullet option to turn the text you just typed into the first item in a bulleted list.

6. Use the on-screen keyboard to hit return and type several more lines. Tapping return always creates a new line in the list. Tapping return a second time ends the list formatting.

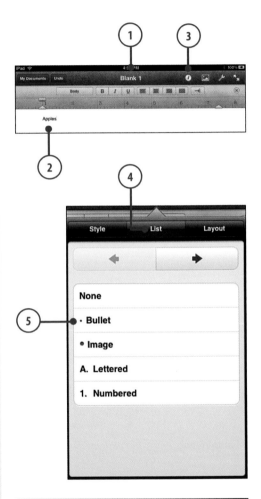

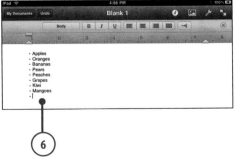

7. Select the entire list.

8. Tap the i button.

9. Tap Numbered to change the list to a numbered list.

10. Tap one line of the list.

11. Tap i again.

12. Tap the right arrow in the List menu to indent the line and create a sublist. You can create sublists as you type or by selecting lines and using the arrow buttons to format after you type.

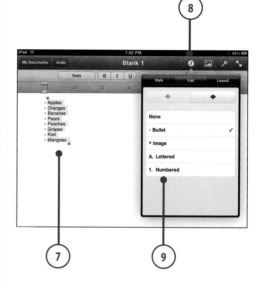

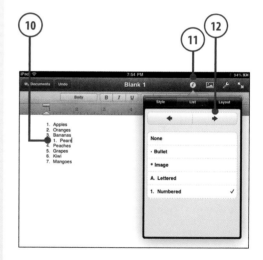

Column Layouts

Pages lets you go beyond boring one-column layouts. You can even change the number of columns for each paragraph.

1. Start a new document and fill it with text—perhaps copy and paste text from a website article.

2. With no text selected, tap the i button.

3. Tap Layout.

Line Spacing

The Layout menu includes duplicates of the alignment buttons and a Line Spacing setting. You can change the line spacing in one-quarter of an inch increments. A change affects the text in the paragraph where the cursor is located or the text in all selected paragraphs.

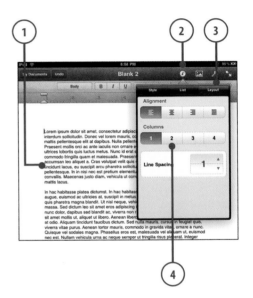

4. Tap 2 under Columns. The entire document changes to a 2-column layout.

5. Tap 1 to switch back to a 1-column layout.

Using Different Column Formats

You can select just one paragraph and apply a two-column layout to it while leaving the rest of your document in one-column layout. Be aware, though, that switching between one column and multiple columns in the same document can yield unpredictable results, so proceed with caution.

Inserting Images

You can place images into your Pages documents. You can even wrap text around the images.

1. Open a new document and fill it with text.

2. Place the cursor somewhere in the text, such as at the beginning of the second paragraph.

3. Tap the Image button.

4. Tap Media.

5. Then select a photo from a photo album.

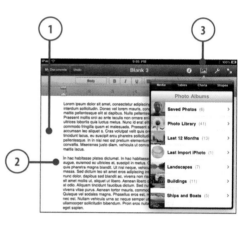

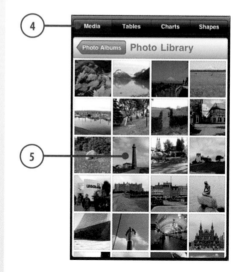

6. The photo appears in the document at the location of the cursor. Tap it to close the menu.

7. You can tap on the image and use Cut, Copy, Delete and Replace on the photo when it is selected. The latter option brings the photos menu back for you to select another.

8. Drag the blue dots around the photo to resize it.

9. While resizing, measurements appear next to the photo.

10. Tap the i button to bring up the Style and Arrange menu.

11. Tap Arrange to see options for flipping a photo, moving it in front of or behind other items on the page, and editing the mask of the photo.

12. Tap Edit Mask.

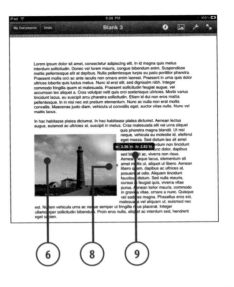

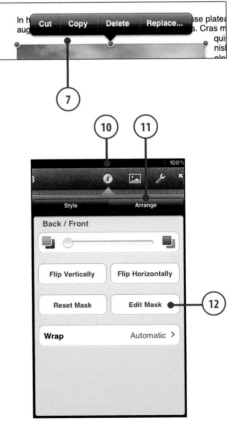

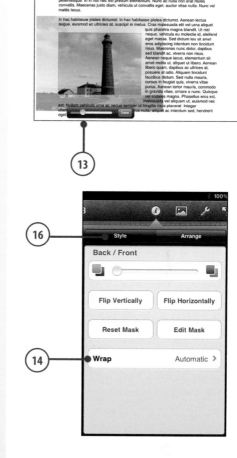

13. Drag the slider to resize the photo. The photo changes size, but the size of the object remains the same, which enables you to put the focus on a particular portion of the photo by moving the photo around inside the space. Tap Done.

14. Tap Wrap.

15. Use the Wrap menu to designate how the text wraps around the photo and whether the photo should stay put on the page or move along as you insert text before it.

16. Tap Style.

17. Choose the type of border that appears around the photo. There are six basic styles to choose from. In addition, you can tap Style Options and chose your own border and effects.

Rearranging Images

After you place an image in your document, you can drag it around and resize it as much as you want. Pages automatically snaps the edges of the image to the margins and center lines of the page as you drag it around.

Importing Clipart

I've found that the best way to get clip art on to your iPad and in to Pages is to drag it into iPhoto. Then, I create a ClipArt event to store the files in. I then sync my iPad, making sure that the ClipArt event is set to sync. You can also do this with a folder if you aren't using iPhoto or are on Windows.

Using Shapes in Documents

In addition to using clip art, you can also use some basic shapes in Pages. Inserting shapes works in the same basic manner.

1. Create a new document and add some text.

2. Tap the Image button to bring up the Media/Tables/Charts/Shapes menu.

3. Tap the Shapes button.

4. Tap a shape, such as the rounded rectangle. It is placed in the middle of the text.

5. Tap the shape in the text to dismiss the menu.

6. Use the blue dots to resize the shape.

7. Tap and drag in the middle of the shape to move it around in the document.

8. Double-tap in the shape to enter text into the shape.

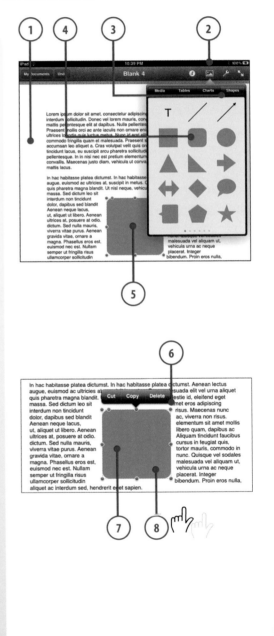

>> Go Further

LOTS OF CHOICES

The first shape, shown with the letter T, is actually a hollow box where you can add text. The next choices are a line, an arrow, and then the shapes you can more easily see.

If you drag to the left, you can look through six pages of shape variations. These are the same shapes but with different borders, shading, or just outlines.

After you select a shape and add it to a document, you can always select it and press the i button to change its style to one of the other five. You can also choose Style Options and specify unique fills, borders, and effects for the shapes.

Creating Tables

Tables are a step up from using lists or tabs to format data in your documents. You can choose from several different types of tables, and entering data into them is relatively easy.

1. Start a new document.

2. Tap the Image button.

3. Tap Tables. There are four different table options. In addition, you can swipe left and right in the menu to reveal six color variations.

4. Tap the first table to insert it.

5. Tap the button to the right of the table or below the table to adjust the number of columns and rows.

6. Double-tap in a cell to enter text.

7. Tap the i button to bring up the Table/Headers/Arrange menu.

8. Tap Table to choose from six table styles.

9. Tap Table Options to go to a menu that gives you even more control over the borders and background colors of the table.

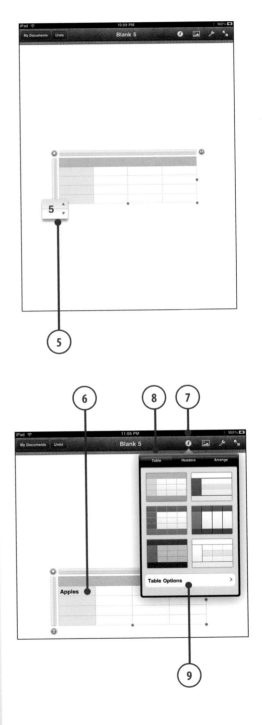

10. Tap Headers to change the number of rows used as a header and the number of columns as well. You can even add footer rows. These all show up as different colors according to the style of table.

11. Tap Arrange to bring up text wrapping options and to send the table behind or in front of other objects.

Moving Tables

You can drag the table around the document by grabbing it at the top, at the left, or by the circle at the top left.

Creating Charts

Charts are another way to express numbers visually. Pages supports nine different kinds of charts.

1. Create a blank document.

2. Tap the Image button.

3. Tap Charts. You can look through six pages of chart styles, but the basics of each set of charts is the same.

4. Tap a chart to select it and insert that type of chart in the middle of your document.

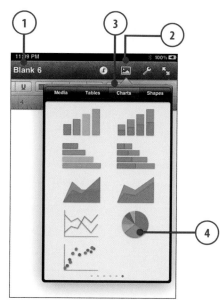

5. Double-tap the chart to bring up the Edit Chart Data screen.

6. Alter the existing data to create your own chart by tapping the field and typing.

7. When you finish entering data, tap Done.

8. When you return to the main document view, select the chart and tap i.

9. From the Chart menu, select a color scheme for the chart.

10. Tap Chart Options. Use the Chart Options menu to change a variety of properties of the chart.

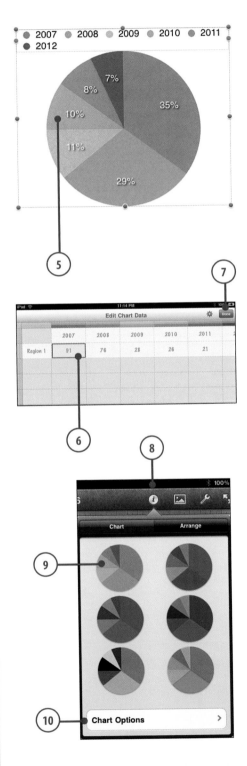

Document Setup

You can change a variety of your document's properties in Pages.

1. Open a document or create a new one.

2. Tap the Wrench button.

3. Choose Document Setup.

4. Drag the arrows at the four edges of the page to adjust the width and height of the page.

5. Tap in the header to add text to the header.

6. While typing in the header, tap the # button to add page numbers to the header.

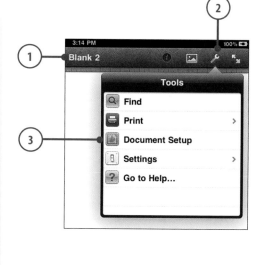

Add Background Images

One thing you can do with Document Setup that is not obvious is to add background objects that appear under every page. You can tap the Image button and add photos, tables, charts, and shapes to the main page area. The image you add appears behind the text. You can even add text that appears on every page by just inserting a borderless, empty text box shape and adding text to it.

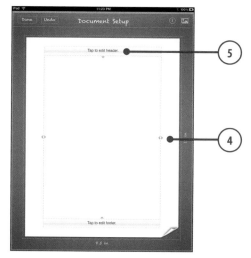

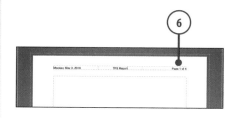

7. Tap the footer to add text to the footer.

8. Tap the page curl to change the paper size.

Create a Background

You can color the entire background by creating a square box and stretching it to fill the page. Then add a shaded or textured background to it as a color in the shape's Style Options. You can also place a picture over the entire background.

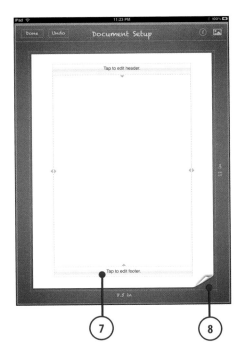

Transferring Documents to Pages with iTunes

When you use Pages on your iPad, you will eventually want to exchange documents with your Mac or PC, which you can do using iTunes.

1. Make sure your iPad and computer are connected via a dock cable.

2. Launch iTunes on your Mac or PC and go to your iPad's Apps page.

3. Scroll down to see the File Sharing Section.

4. Click Pages in the list on the left.

5. Click Add to import files into your iPad, or drag and drop them.

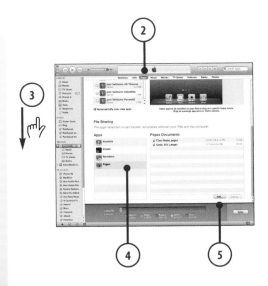

Pages Does Word

You can put more than just Pages documents into the iTunes list to import. Pages can also take Microsoft Word .doc and even .docx files.

6. On your iPad, launch Pages.

7. Tap the Copy button while browsing your documents and then tap Copy from iTunes.

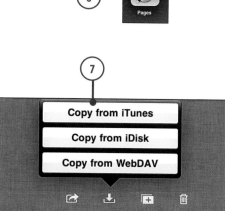

8. Select the document to bring in to Pages. At this point you see a progress bar appear as the file is imported.

Pages Is Not Pages

The Pages on your iPad and the Pages on your Mac are not the same. You can do a lot more with Pages on your Mac. So sometimes you might receive a Document Import Warning message telling you what didn't work as you import your file to your iPad.

Get It From the Cloud

You can also copy Pages documents from MobileMe's storage space iDisk and from any WebDAV server on the Internet. This makes it possible to transfer documents even without attaching your iPad to your computer.

Transferring Documents from Pages to iTunes

You can also go the other way and get documents from Pages on your iPad back to your Mac or PC via iTunes.

1. Make sure your iPad and computer are connected via a dock cable.

2. While browsing your documents, choose the one you want to export and tap the Boxed Arrow button.

3. Choose Copy to iDisk. Alternatively, you can choose one of the many other sharing destinations, such as iWork.com, iDisk, or Email.

4. Choose Pages if you use Pages on a Mac. Otherwise, choose Word if you use Microsoft Word in Windows. Choose PDF to send a noneditable document to your computer for distribution or printing.

5. The document takes a few seconds to export and then appears in your Pages Documents under File Sharing in the Apps section of iTunes.

Other Ways to Transfer Documents

You can also transfer documents via email and Apple's iWork.com service (if you have an account). You can use this with the same file transfer process with Numbers and Keynote. There are also some third-party apps that use iTunes to transfer files.

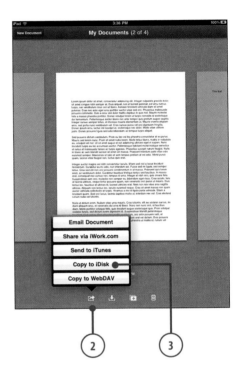

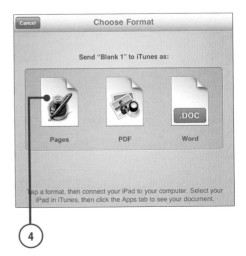

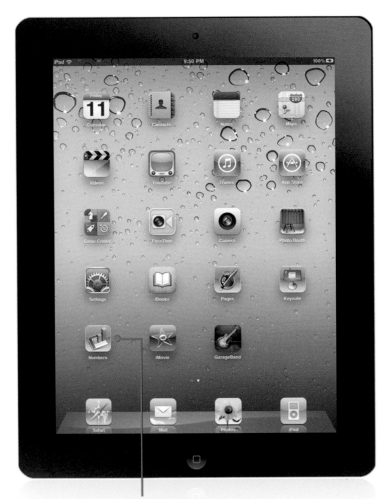

Design and enter data
into spreadsheets.

With Numbers you can create data spreadsheets, perform calculations, and create forms and charts.

12

→ Creating a New Spreadsheet
→ Totaling Columns
→ Averaging Columns
→ Performing Math
→ Formatting Tables
→ Creating Forms
→ Creating Charts
→ Using Multiple Tables

Spreadsheets with Numbers

Numbers is a versatile program that enables you to create the most boring table of numbers ever (feel free to try for the world record on that one) or an elegant chart that illustrates a point like no paragraph of text ever could.

Creating a New Spreadsheet

The way you manage documents in Numbers is exactly the same as you do in Pages, so if you need a refresher, refer to Chapter 11, "Writing with Pages." Let's jump right in to creating a simple spreadsheet.

1. Tap the Numbers icon on your Home screen to start.

2. Tap New Spreadsheet to see all the template choices.

3. Tap Blank to choose the most basic template.

Numbers Terminology

A grid of numbers is called a *table*. A page of tables, often just a single table taking up the whole page, is a *sheet*. You can have multiple sheets in a document, all represented by tabs. The first tab in this case represents "Sheet 1." Tap the + to add a new sheet.

4. Tap in one of the cells to select the sheet. An outline appears around the cell.

5. Double-tap the cell this time. An on-screen keypad appears.

6. Use the keypad to type a number. The number appears in both the cell and a text field above the keypad. Use this text field to edit the text, tapping inside it to reposition the cursor if necessary.

7. Tap the upper next button, the one with the arrow pointing right.

Switching Keyboard Options

The four buttons just above and to the left of the keypad represent number, time, text, and formula formats for cells. If you select the number, you get a keypad to enter a number. If you select the clock, you get a special keypad to enter dates and times. If you select the T, you get a regular keyboard. Finally, if you select the equal sign (=) , you get a keypad and special buttons to enter formulas.

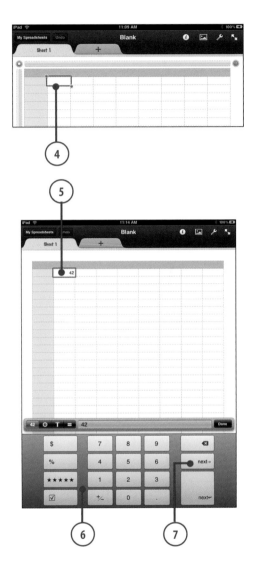

8. The cursor moves to the column in the next cell. Type a number here, too.

9. Tap the next button again and enter a third number.

10. Tap the space just above the first number you entered. The keypad changes to a standard keyboard to type text instead of numbers.

11. Type a label for this first column.

12. Tap in each of the other two column heads to enter titles for them as well.

13. Tap to the left of the first number you entered. Type a row title.

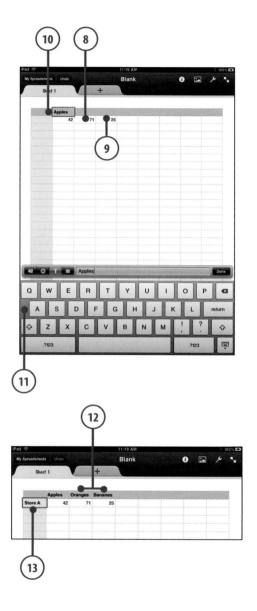

14. Now enter a few more rows of data.

15. Tap the Done button.

16. Tap and drag the circle with four dots in it to the right of the bar above the table. Drag it to the left to remove the unneeded columns.

17. Tap and drag the same circle at the bottom of the vertical bar to the right of the table. Drag it up to remove most of the extra columns, leaving a few for future use.

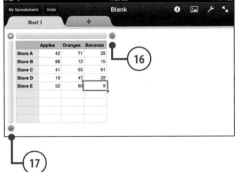

Totaling Columns

One of the most basic formula types is a sum. In the previous example, for instance, you might want to total each column.

1. Start with the result of the previous example. Double-tap in the cell just below the bottom number in the first column.

2. Tap the = button to switch to the formula keypad.

3. Tap the SUM button on the keypad.

4. The formula for the cell appears in the text field.

5. Tap the green check mark button.

6. The result of the formula appears in the cell. Repeat steps 2 through 4 for the other columns in the table.

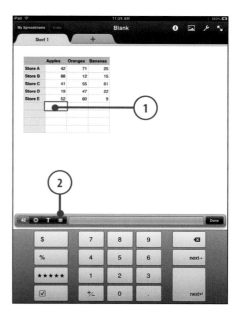

Automatic Updates

If you are not familiar with spreadsheets, the best thing about them is that formulas like this automatically update. So if you change the number of Apples in Store C in the table, the sum in the last row automatically changes to show the new total.

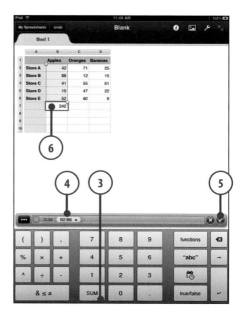

Averaging Columns

We lucked out a bit with the sum function because it has its own button. But what about the other hundreds of functions? Let's start with something simple like column averages.

1. Continuing with the example from the previous section, double-tap on the cell below the total of the first column of numbers.

2. Tap the = button to switch to formula mode.

3. Tap the functions button.

4. Tap Statistical from the Functions button menu. Tap the Categories tab at the top of the menu if Recent is selected instead.

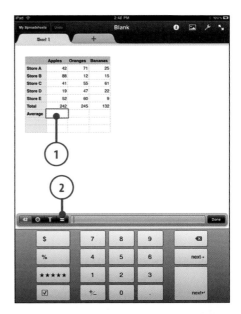

5. Tap AVERAGE from the list of functions.

6. Now you get AVERAGE(value) in the entry field. The light blue means the "value" is selected and ready to be defined.

7. Tap cell B2 (Apples for Store A).

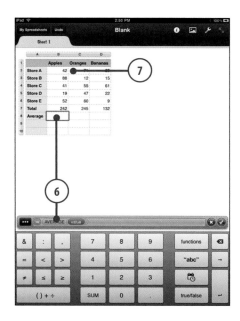

8. Drag the bottom dot to include cells B2 through B6. Don't add the Total row to the average. The entry field should now read AVERAGE(B2:B6).

9. Tap the green check mark button.

10. The average of the column should now be in the cell. Tap it once to see the Cut/Copy/Paste menu.

11. Tap Copy.

12. Tap the cell below the total for the second column of numbers.

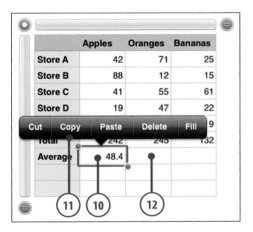

13. Drag the bottom-right dot to expand the area to cover the next cell as well.

14. Double-tap in the two cells to bring up the Paste option.

15. Tap Paste.

16. Tap Paste Formulas.

17. All three columns now show the average for rows 2 through 6. Notice how Numbers is smart enough to understand when you copy and paste a formula from one column to the other, that it should look at the same rows but a different column.

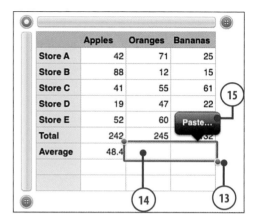

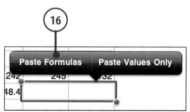

Performing Calculations

So far we have seen two simple formulas. Let's see what else you can do with one of hundreds of different functions and the standard mathematical symbols.

1. Start with a table like this one. It shows the base and height measurements for three triangles.

2. Double-tap in the third column.

3. Tap the = button to enter a formula.

4. Tap the first number in the first column. "Base Triangle 1" should fill the entry field.

5. Tap the division symbol.

6. Tap the 2.

7. Tap the Multiplication button.

8. Tap the first number in the second column.

9. The entry field now reads "Base Triangle 1 ÷ 2 x Height Triangle 1."

10. Tap the green check mark.

11. You get the result of 10.5, which is half the base of the triangle times its height, or the area of the triangle.

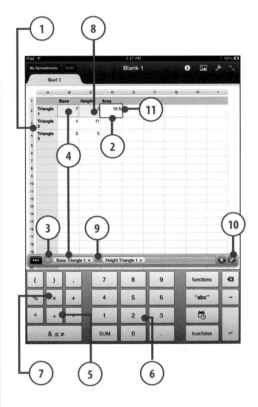

Using Parentheses

Note that a more careful mathematician would rather see it written "(Base Triangle 1 ÷ 2) × Height Triangle 1." By grouping the base divided by 2 inside parentheses, you guarantee the correct result. You can use the parentheses to do that in the formula keypad.

Formatting Tables

Let's move away from calculations to design. You have many formatting options to make your spreadsheets pretty.

Formatting Cells

1. Go back to the original example or something similar.

2. Select the six cells that make up the totals and average.

3. Tap the i button.

4. Tap Cells to see cell styling, formatting, and coloring choices.

5. Select Fill Color.

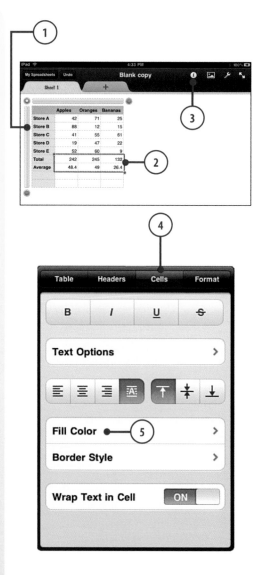

6. Tap the lightest shade of blue. You can also drag to the left to go to the second page of colors, which is actually a set of grays. The second page includes an option to reset the fill to the original style.

7. Tap the back arrow to go back to the Cells menu.

8. Tap B to make the text bold.

9. Change the selection to include only the row of averages.

10. Tap the i button again.

11. Tap Text Options.

12. Tap Color.

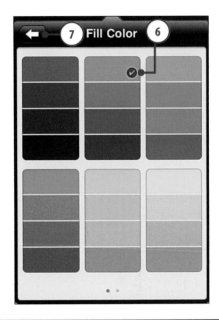

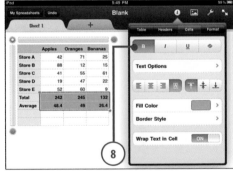

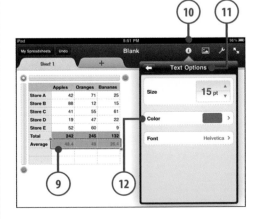

13. Choose the third darkest blue.

14. Tap the back arrow.

15. Tap Format.

16. Tap the blue arrow to the right of Number.

17. Set the number of decimal places. Try 2.

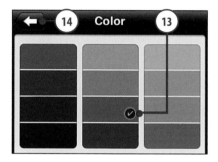

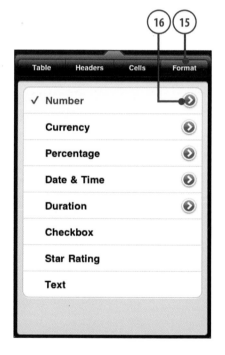

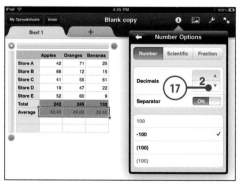

Formatting Whole Tables

Beyond just formatting cells, you can also use many options to change the basic style of your table. Let's explore some of the options.

1. Starting with the table from the previous example; tap anywhere in the table to select it.

2. Tap the i button to bring up the menu.

3. Tap Table.

4. Try a different style, like the greenish one on the left, second down.

5. The new style replaces the formatting we did for the cells, so it is best to find a table style before you customize the cell styles.

6. Tap the Table Options button to explore other table options.

7. Tap the Table Name switch to add or remove the title.

8. Tap the Table Border switch to add or remove a border.

9. Tap the Alternating Rows switch to have the color of the rows alternate.

10. Tap Grid Options for more detailed control of the look of the grid used in the table.

11. Tap Text Size and Table Font to change the size and font used in the table.

Using Headers and Footers

Let's continue with the previous example to explore headers and footers:

1. Tap the Back button to return to the previous menu.

2. Tap the Headers button to adjust the number of header rows and columns and add footer rows.

3. Tap the Footer Rows up arrow to increase the footer rows to 4.

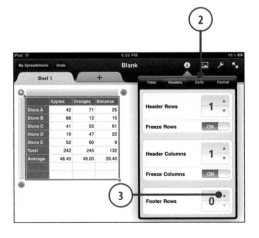

Creating Forms

Forms are an alternative way to enter data in a spreadsheet. A form contains many pages, each page representing a row in a table. Let's continue with the previous example and use it to make a form.

1. Tap the + button, which looks like a second tab in the document.

2. Tap New Form.

3. Choose a table. We have only one, so the choice is simple. Tap Table 1 to see the first page in the form, which represents the first row of data from our table.

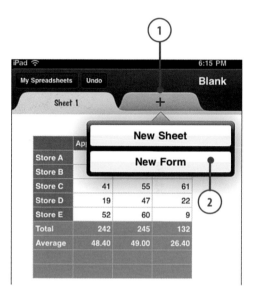

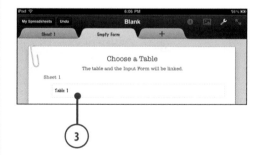

4. Tap the right arrow at the bottom of the screen to move through the five existing rows (pages) of data.

5. Tap the + button at the bottom of the screen to enter a new row of data.

6. Tap at the top of the screen to enter a row heading.

7. Tap in each of the three fields to enter data.

8. Use the next button on the on-screen keypad to move to the next field.

9. When you finish, tap the first tab, Sheet 1, to return to the original spreadsheet. You should see the new data in a new row.

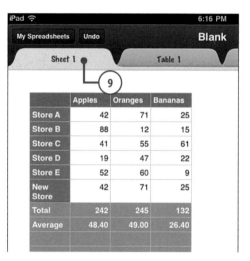

It's Not All Good

WHY DIDN'T THE FORMULAS UPDATE?

Unfortunately, the formulas for the totals and averages in our example did not update to use the new row. They both stuck with rows 2 through 7 of the table and did not expand to use row 8. What went wrong?

Well, first, if we had added a row in the middle of the table, it would have expanded the sum area. So part of our problem is that we added a cell below the sum area.

Second, we created the cell with the sum function in a regular cell. Then we turned it into a footer cell. If we start over by deleting that sum cell and creating it again, Numbers is smart enough to realize that we mean *all* the rows in the column between the header and footer. Instead of =SUM(B2:B7) we would simply get =SUM(B). Then we can add more rows using the form, and the sum would increase properly.

So delete the formula from B9 and replace it with =SUM(B), and you are in business. Do the same with the other sum and average cells. When you do this, Numbers is smart enough to create the formula for you when you tap the SUM button. The formula is actually stated as =SUM(Apples) because we named the column Apples.

To create your Average row, use the Functions button and select AVERAGE as before, but tap the bar above columns B, C, and D to tell Numbers you want the average of the whole column between the header and footer.

Creating Charts

Representing numbers visually is one of the primary functions of a modern spreadsheet program. With Numbers, you can create bar, line, and pie charts and many variations of each.

1. Create a new blank spreadsheet and then fill it with some basic data to use as an example. Shrink the table to remove unneeded cells.

2. Tap the Image button at the top of the screen.

3. Select Charts.

4. Page through six different chart color variations. Tap the first chart, the one at the top left.

5. Double-tap the chart.

6. Tap and drag over all the numbers in the body of your table to add all the rows of data to the table.

7. Tap Done.

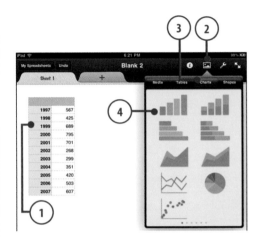

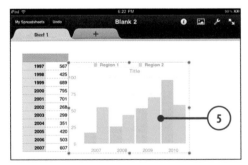

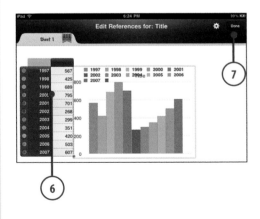

8. Tap and drag the chart and position it on the sheet.

9. Tap on the chart to make sure it is selected.

10. Tap the i button. Notice that you can alter all sorts of properties using the Chart/X Axis/Y Axis and Arrange menu.

11. Tap Chart Options.

12. Tap Chart Type.

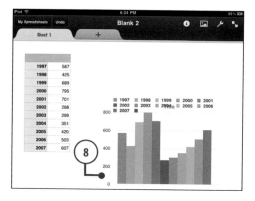

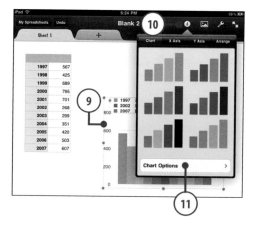

13. Tap Line to change the chart type to a line graph.

14. Tap outside the menu to dismiss it.

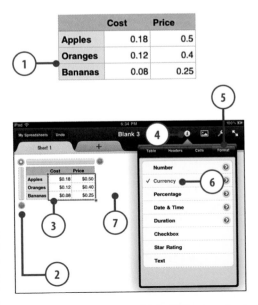

Using Multiple Tables

The primary way Numbers differs from spreadsheet programs such as Excel is that Numbers emphasizes page design. A Numbers sheet is not meant to contain just one grid of numbers. In Numbers you can use multiple tables.

1. Create a new, blank spreadsheet and fill it with data as in the example image.

2. Shrink the table to remove any unneeded cells.

3. Select the cells in the body.

4. Tap the i button.

5. Tap Format.

6. Tap Currency.

7. Tap outside the menu to dismiss it.

8. Tap the table to select it. Make sure just the table as a whole is selected, not a cell.

Selecting a Table

It can be difficult to select an entire table without selecting a cell. Tap in a cell to select it. Then tap the circle that appears in the upper-left corner of the table to change your selection to the entire table.

9. Tap the i button.

10. Tap Table Options.

11. Tap the Table Name switch to give the table a name.

12. Tap outside the menu to dismiss it.

13. Select just the table name and change it.

14. Tap the Image button.

15. Tap Tables.

16. Select the first table type.

17. Enter the data as shown and shrink the table to remove any unneeded cells.

18. Select the table title and change it.

Clean Up the Formatting

To keep this tutorial short, I left some things out. For instance, you can select the date columns and change the formatting. Obviously each row represents a month. So you don't need the full date, including the day. You can change the date format of those columns to one that doesn't include the day, only the month and year. Just select those cells and tap the i button and look under Format. Select Date & Time and tap the blue circle to choose a specific date and time format.

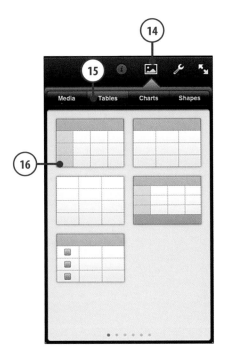

Cost and Price

	Cost	Price
Apples	$0.18	$0.50
Oranges	$0.12	$0.40
Bananas	$0.08	$0.25

Inventory Received

	Apples	Oranges	Bananas
Jan 1, 2010	50	0	0
Feb 1, 2010	50	100	200
Mar 1, 2010	0	200	0
Apr 1, 2010	50	0	200

19. Select the entire second table.

20. Tap the Copy button.

21. Tap outside the table in a new location in the sheet.

22. Tap Paste.

23. Change the title and contents of the new table as shown.

24. Now select the second and third tables and expand them with one extra column each, as shown.

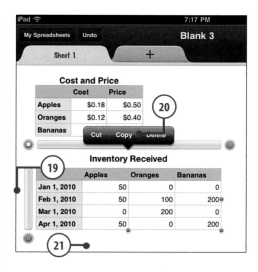

25. Double-tap in the first cell under Cost.

26. Tap on the = button next to the entry field to enter a formula.

27. Tap the Apples cell for the first row.

28. Tap × in the on-screen keyboard, and tap the cost of apples from the Cost and Price table.

29. Tap +.

30. Tap the oranges cell and then tap × again. Then tap the cost of oranges and again tap +.

31. Tap the Bananas cell. Then tap × and tap the cost of bananas.

32. Tap the part of the formula that reads Cost Apples.

33. Turn on all four preservation switches to prevent the cell reference from changing as we copy and paste. We want the amount of inventory to change with each row, but the price from the other table remains the same.

34. Repeat steps 32 and 33 for the cost of oranges and the cost of bananas in the formula.

35. Tap the green check mark to complete the formula.

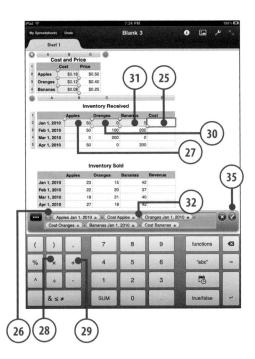

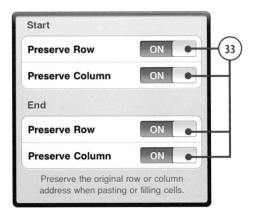

36. Tap the i button.

37. Change the format of the cell to Currency.

38. Copy that cell and paste it in to the three below it. When prompted, choose to Paste Formulas not Values.

The result is that you have a calculation based on data from two tables. You can complete this spreadsheet if you want. Create a similar formula for the revenue column of the next table, based on the price of each item and the amount sold.

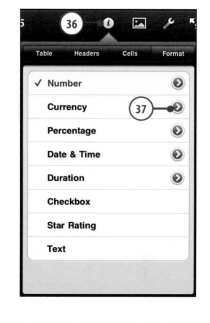

Enhance the Sheet

Another thing you can do is to add more titles, text, and images to the sheet—even shapes and arrows. These not only make the sheet look nice, but can also act as documentation as a reminder of what you need to do each month—or instruct someone else what to do to update the sheet.

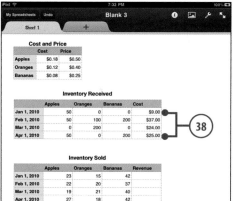

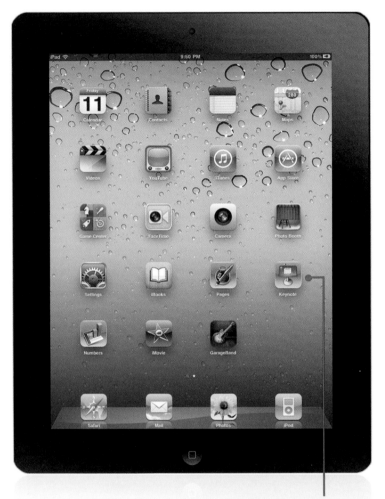

Create and display business and
educational presentations.

In this chapter we use Keynote to build and display presentations.

→ Building a Simple Presentation

→ Building Your Own Slide

→ Adding Transitions

→ Organizing Slides

→ Playing Your Presentation

→ Presenting on an External Display

Presentations with Keynote

You can't have a suite of business apps without having a Presentation tool, and Keynote is that tool on the iPad. The basics of using Keynote are the same as for Pages and Numbers. So let's get right to making presentations.

Building a Simple Presentation

Keynote works only in horizontal screen orientation. So after you launch Keynote, turn your iPad on its side.

1. Tap the Keynote icon on the Home screen. If this is the first time you are using Keynote, the sample presentation should be front and center.

2. Tap the + button to create a new presentation.

3. Tap New Presentation.

4. Choose a theme. We use Gradient for the task.

5. Double-tap the line of text that reads Double-tap to edit.

6. Type a title using the on-screen keyboard.

7. Tap the subtitle area and type a subtitle.

8. Tap the Close Keyboard button.

9. Tap the small button in the bottom-right corner of the picture to open a photo albums browser.

10. Choose a photo.

11. Tap the large + button at the bottom-left corner to bring up a list of slides.

12. Tap any of the slides templates to add a slide. You now have two slides in your presentation.

Go Further

STARTING NEW PRESENTATIONS

Keynote presentations are made up of slides. The slides in the current presentation are shown at the left of the screen. The selected slide takes up most of the screen. The slides are built from one of eight slide templates, which you can modify as needed.

Be aware that there is no way to switch themes or to access the design of another theme after you start a new presentation. If you're used to working with Keynote on a Mac, you might be disappointed by this.

You can copy and paste entire slides between presentation documents, though. So if you want a document that mixes themes, you can achieve it by copying and pasting.

Building Your Own Slide

You can remove items and add your own to any template. We can practice adding your own elements to a slide by using the blank template.

1. Start a new document or continue from the previous example. Tap + to add a new slide.

2. Choose the blank slide to the lower right.

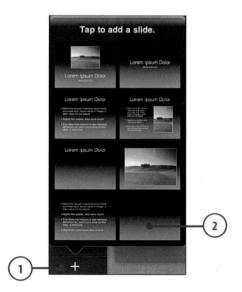

3. Tap the Image button at the top to add an element.

4. Tap Media.

5. Select an album, and then select a photo from that album.

6. With the photo selected, grab one of the blue dots and shrink the image.

7. With the image selected, tap the i button and then tap Style.

8. Tap the bottom right of the six basic image styles or tap Style Options to customize the look of the photo even more.

Select All

To select all objects, tap a space with no objects. After a short delay, tap there again, and then you can choose Select All.

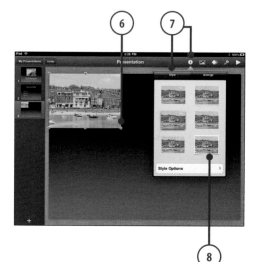

9. Add two more images using steps 3 through 8.

10. To select multiple items, use two fingers. Tap the first image with one finger and hold it. Use a second figure to tap the other two images to add them to the selection. Then drag all three images into a better position.

11. Tap the Image button to add another element.

Tables and Charts Anyone?

You can also add tables and charts, even basic shapes, in the same way you would do it in Pages. There are a lot of similarities between using Pages and using Keynote.

12. Tap Shapes.

13. Tap the first element, a T, which represents a plain text box.

14. Tap outside the menu to dismiss it.

15. Tap the text box to select it.

16. Drag it to a new position and expand it.

17. Double-tap in the text box to enter some text.

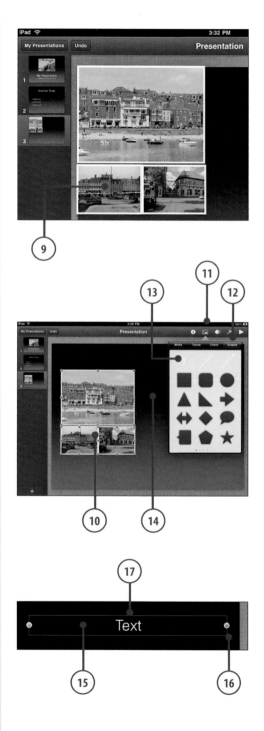

18. With the text selected, tap the i button.

19. Tap Text to change the font style.

20. Make the text bold by tapping B.

21. Tap outside the menu to dismiss it.

22. Your text is now bold.

Adding Transitions

Just like other presentation programs, Keynote on iPad has a number of transition options. To practice working with transitions, start with a sample presentation, such as the one we have been working on, or create a new document with some sample slides.

1. Select the first slide on the left.

2. Tap the Transitions button (two diamonds overlapping).

3. Tap the blue circle to pick a transition.

4. Scroll through the transitions and pick one. Try Cube. The slide animates to show you the transition. It then returns.

5. Tap Options.

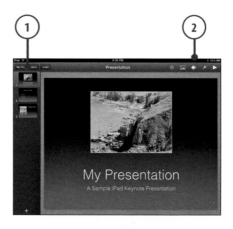

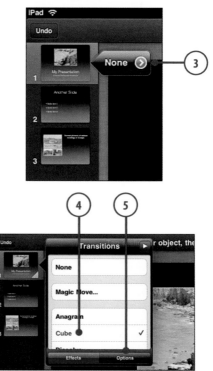

6. Select any options associated with the transition. For example, a Cube transition can move in any of four directions. If you don't want to change any options, tap elsewhere to dismiss the menu.

7. Tap Done in the upper-right corner of the screen.

Magic Move

Another type of transition is the Magic Move. This is where objects on one slide are the same as the objects on the next, but they are in different positions. The transition between the slides moves these objects from the first position to the second.

1. Select a slide with several objects on it, such as three images. Tap the Transitions button.

2. Tap the blue button to choose a transition.

3. Choose Magic Move.

Unique Effects with Magic Move

The great thing about the Magic Move transition is that you can create some unique effects. For instance, in the example, I could bunch all the photos into a tiny space on the first slide and then spread them out in the second slide. The transition would make it seem like the photos are bursting out and falling into place.

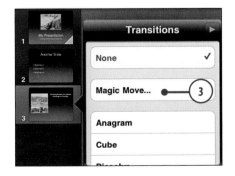

4. Tap Yes to duplicate the current slide so that you have two identical slides from which to create the Magic Move transition.

5. Slides 3 and 4 are identical, and slide 4 is the current slide. Move the objects around to reposition them or resize them. The stars indicate which elements are taking part in the magic move.

6. Tap the third frame.

7. Tap the play arrow to preview the transition from slide 3 to slide 4.

8. Tap Done in the upper-right corner of the screen.

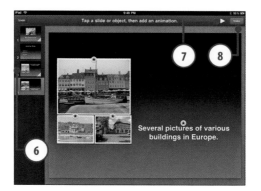

Object Transitions

In addition to the entire screen trans-
forming from one slide to the next,
you can also define how you want
individual elements on the slide to
appear.

1. Start off with a slide that includes
   a title and a bullet list. Tap the
   Transitions button.

2. Tap the slide's title text.

3. Tap the build in button.

4. Tap Blast to see a preview of the
   animation. You can also explore
   the Options, Delivery, and Order
   parts of the menu, but for this
   task we leave those settings
   alone.

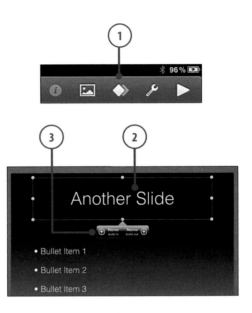

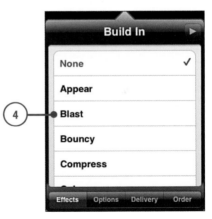

5. Tap the bullet list.

6. Tap build in.

7. Scroll down to Move In and tap it.

8. Tap Delivery.

Don't Build the First Object

A common mistake is to set every object to build, as we have in this example. Because the first object, the title, builds in, it means that nothing appears on the slide at first. You start off blank. Then the title appears and then the bullet items. Sometimes, though, you should start a slide with the title already on it.

---

9. Tap By Bullet and then tap Done in the upper-right corner of the screen. The effect works by first showing you a blank screen, and then when you tap, the title appears with the Blast transition. Each of your next three taps makes a bullet appear.

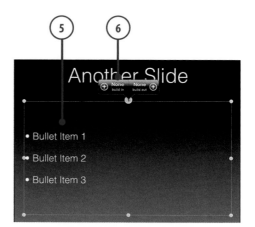

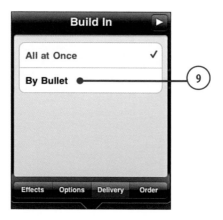

Organizing Slides

As you create presentations on your iPad, you might discover you need to re-order your slides, but that's no problem with Notes. To practice, use a presentation that has several slides.

1. Create a presentation that includes several slides.

2. Tap and hold the third slide. It grows slightly larger and begins to follow your finger so that you can drag it between slides 1 and 2.

Grouping Slides

There are two options when you drag a slide and place it back in the list. The first is to place it flush left, where it inserts normally. If you move the slide slightly to the right, though, you are grouping the slide with the one above it. Groups are a great way to put slides that belong together as a single element. That way you can move them as one unit if you need to.

3. Drag slide 4 so it inserts in a group owned by slide 2.

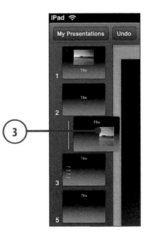

4. Tap the triangle on the left of slide 2 to close the group.

5. Tap slide 5 with your finger and continue to hold.

6. Use your other hand to tap slides 6 and 7 and then release your finger. You can now move this group of three slides as one unit.

7. Tap once to select a slide. Then tap a second time after a short delay to bring up a menu.

8. Use Cut, Copy, and Paste as you would while editing text. You can duplicate slides this way.

9. Tap Delete to remove a slide.

10. Tap Skip to mark a slide as one to skip during the presentation. This comes in handy when you want to remove a slide from a presentation temporarily, perhaps while presenting to a specific audience.

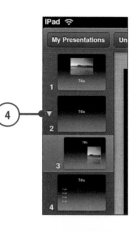

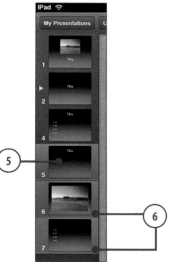

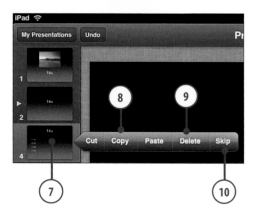

Playing Your Presentation

After you create your presentation, or if you want to preview what you've done, you can play your presentation.

1. With a presentation open in Keynote, tap the Play button.

2. The presentation fills the screen. Tap on the center or right side of the screen to advance to the next slide. You can also tap and drag from left to right.

3. To go back to the previous slide, drag right to left.

4. Tap on the left edge of the screen to bring up a list of slides.

5. Tap one of the items in the list to go directly to that slide.

6. Double-tap in the list of slides to dismiss the list.

7. Double-tap in the center of the screen to end the presentation and return to editing mode.

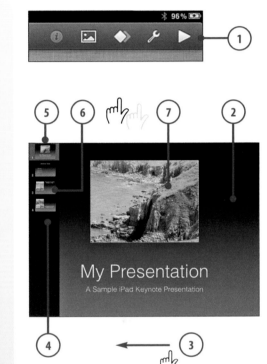

Presenting on an External Display

Presenting on your iPad with people looking over your shoulder probably isn't your goal. You want to present on a large monitor or a projector, which you can do with an iPad Dock Connector to VGA Adapter (see Chapter 18, "iPad Accessories," for more information).

1. When you have your VGA adapter connected, the Play button has a box around it to indicate that your iPad is ready to present on an external video device. Tap the Play button.

2. Tap in the middle or right side of the screen to move forward to the next slide or build the next object on the current slide.
3. Tap the left edge of the screen to bring up a list of slides.

4. Tap on one of the slides on the left to jump to it.
5. Tap the X button to stop the presentation.

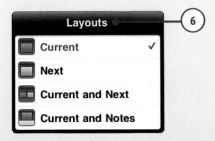

6. Tap the Layouts button to bring up different layout options. You can choose to view both the current slide and next slide or the current slide with your slide notes at the bottom.

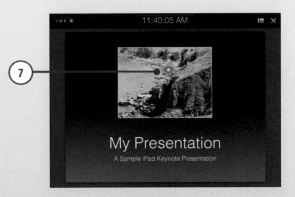

7. Tap and hold your finger on the slide to bring up a red dot that you can use as a pointer.

Make Sure Your iPad Is Charged!

Video adapters fit in to your iPad's dock, which means, with the exception of the HDMI adapter, you can't use the dock to hook your iPad up to a power source while you are presenting. If you plan to give a long presentation and are short on battery power, you might be in trouble. Make sure you have a near fully charged iPad if you plan to use it to present this way.

WHICH VIDEO ADAPTER?

>> Go Further

Although the only way to get Keynote's presentation out to an external screen is to use an adapter, there are two main choices: the VGA adapter or the HDMI adapter. Get the VGA adapter if you plan to present over a traditional meeting room projector. However, newer televisions and maybe some advanced projectors would use an HDMI connection. You can also convert VGA to fit other video connections. For instance, if you need to connect to a TV using a component or s-video, you should find some VGA adapters that work. See if you can find one that has been verified to work with an iPad before buying.

Search for locations or
get directions with Maps.

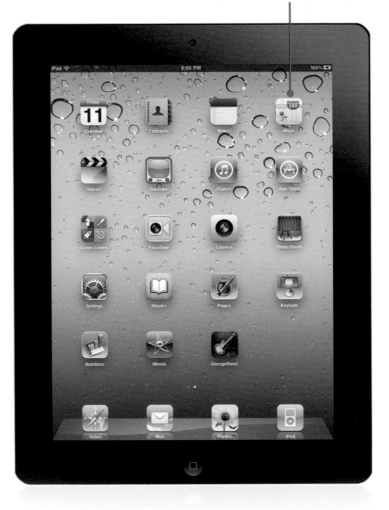

In this chapter, you learn to use the Maps app to find locations and get directions.

→ Finding a Location

→ Searching for Places

→ Getting Directions

→ Setting Bookmarks

→ Using Views

→ Getting Traffic Reports

14

Navigating with Maps

The Maps app is a great way to plan a trip—whether you're going to the grocery store or across the country. Maps is basically an interface to Google Maps that gives you map and satellite views and street-level panoramic views and enables you to search for locations, get directions, and much more.

Finding a Location

The simplest thing you can probably do with Maps is to find a location.

1. Tap the Maps app on your Home screen.

2. Tap the Search button.

3. Tap in the Search or Address field.

4. Type the name of a place.

5. Tap the Search button on the on-screen keyboard.

What Can You Search For?

You can search for a specific address. You can also use a general time or the name of a place or person, and Maps does the best it can to locate it. For example, you can try three-letter airport codes, landmark names, street intersections, and building names. The search keeps in mind your current Maps view, so if you search for a general area first, such as Denver, CO, and then for a building name, it attempts to find the building in Denver before looking elsewhere in the world.

6. The map shifts to that location and zooms in.

7. Tap the i button next to the location name to get more information.

8. Use the Add to Contacts button to add the name, address, phone number, and other information to your Contacts app.

9. Use the Share Location button to email a contact (.vcf file) of the location to someone.

10. Use the Add to Bookmarks button to add the location as a bookmark in the Maps app.

11. Tap outside the information area and try dragging and pinching to get a feel for using Maps.

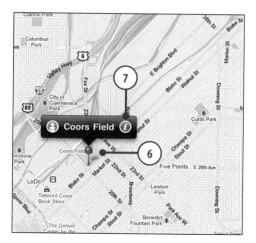

Where Am I?

Want to quickly center the map on your current location? Tap the GPS button (it looks like a compass arrow) at the top of the screen. Even if your iPad doesn't have a GPS receiver, it takes a good guess as to your current location based on the local Wi-Fi networks it can see.

Searching for Places and Things

You can also use Maps to search for something that has more than one location. For instance, you could search for one location of your favorite computer store.

1. Start in Maps. You should see the last area you were viewing. If it is not your current location, search for that location or press the GPS button to go there.

2. Tap the search field and type the name of a store.

3. Tap the Search button on the on-screen keyboard.

4. Red pins appear on the map for all locations matching the search term in the general area. You might also see some dots representing other potential locations.

5. Tap a red pin to get the name of the location and an i button for more info.

Sometimes Being General Is Good

Don't always restrict yourself to specific names such as "Apple store." You can type in general terms such as "coffee" or "restaurant" to get a broader selection of results.

Sometimes It Gets It Wrong

The Google maps database is huge, which means it also contains errors. Sometimes an address is wrong or the information is out of date, so you find yourself in front of a shoe shop instead of your favorite restaurant.

Getting Directions

Although the Maps app is not the equivalent of some turn-by-turn GPS devices, it does offer detailed directions to get you from one point to another.

1. In Maps, tap the Directions button. At this point, you may be asked to confirm whether the Maps app is allowed to use your current location.

2. Two fields appear at the top right. The left field is already filled in with your current location. Change the location by tapping the X in the field to clear it and typing a new address.

3. Tap in the second field and type the destination location.

4. Tap the Search button on the on-screen keyboard.

5. The directions show up as a blue line on the map. You might need to pinch to zoom out to see the whole route.

6. Change the route for driving directions, public transportation options, and walking directions.

7. Tap the Start button to go through the route turn-by-turn.

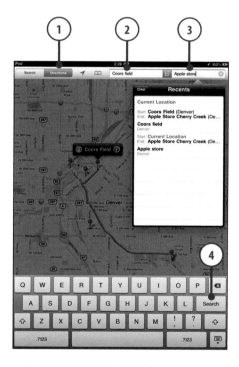

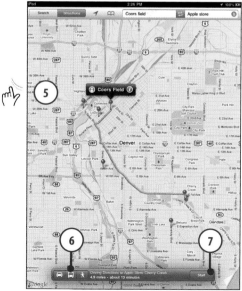

8. Tap the right arrow inside the blue bar to look at the first step of the trip. Keep tapping the right arrow to go through each step.

9. Tap the List button to the left side of the blue bar to view the directions in a route overview.

10. Tap any of the steps in the route to jump to it on the map.

More Complex Routes

Sadly the Maps app won't let you have more than two waypoints for a route. And you can't tap in the middle of a route. Fortunately, Google maps also works fine in the Safari browser on your iPad. So you can always browse to http://maps.google.com and work with maps there.

Setting Bookmarks

If you find yourself requesting directions to or from the same location often, you might want to set a bookmark for that spot.

1. In Maps, search for a location.

2. Tap the i button to bring up the info box on that location.

3. Tap Add to Bookmarks.

4. Edit the name for the location if you want.

5. Tap Save.

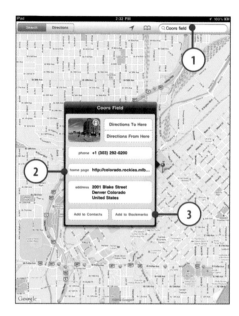

6. Tap the Bookmarks button at the top of the screen to view your bookmarks.

7. At the bottom of the Bookmarks menu, tap Recents or Contacts to see a list of recently visited locations or pull up the address stored for a contact.

8. Tap the name of a bookmark to go to that location on the map.

9. You can also tap Edit to remove bookmarks.

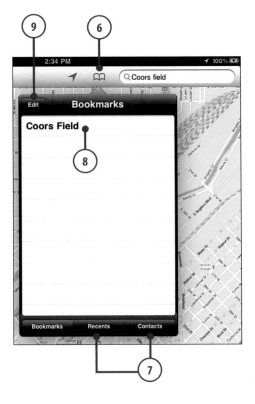

Add a Bookmark Manually

You can also create a bookmark by manually dropping a pin on the map. Tap and hold any location on the map, and a purple pin appears there. You can then drag the pin to another location if it isn't placed exactly where you want it. These pins have addresses and an i button just like any searched-for location. So you can use the Add to Bookmarks button after tapping the i to add it as a bookmark. This comes in handy when Google doesn't quite get the address right.

Using Views

One of the coolest things about online maps are the satellite and street views. Both are fun and helpful and a lot more interesting than a traditional map.

Using Satellite View

Satellite view is like the Classic Map view in that you can search for places and get directions.

1. In Maps, tap the bottom-right corner, where the map page is curled a bit.

2. Tap Satellite to see a satellite view of your location. If that view isn't quite what you need, select Hybrid to see a satellite view that also gives you map references to identify items on the map.

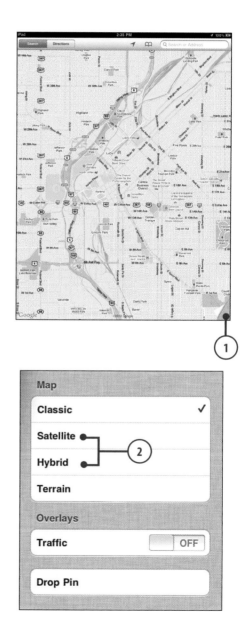

3. Unpinch in the center of the map to zoom in.

4. The closer view helps show you what the streets actually look like.

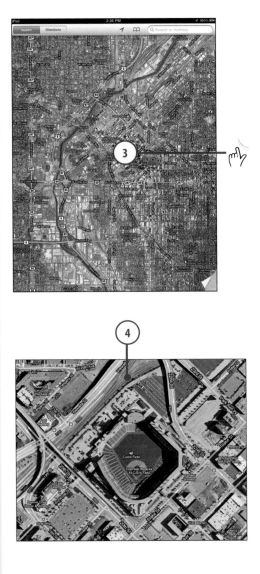

Using Street View

1. Start by looking in Maps using the Normal Classic view.

2. Tap and hold on a spot in the map, preferably on a major street, until a pin drops.

3. Tap the i button.

4. If the information box includes an orange circle with a head and shoulder icon, you can go to Street view at this spot. Tap the picture or the icon.

Not in My Town

Although Street view is great for those of us who live in big cities, it isn't available for every location. For there to be a Street view image, a Google car has to pass down your street at some point to take pictures. They've gotten to a lot of streets but not everywhere.

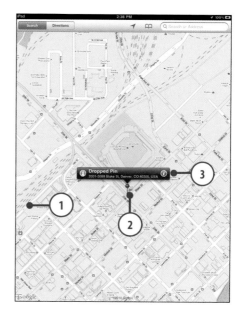

5. The whole screen is taken over by a panoramic image. Drag left and right to look around 360 degrees. Pinch to zoom in and out. Note the mini map at the bottom right with an indicator that shows which direction you are looking.

6. Turn to look down a street so you can see the street name and an arrow. Tap the arrow to move to the next panoramic image along the street.

7. Tap the mini map to return to the Classic Map view.

What's It Good For?

You might wonder what the purpose of Street view is. Well, suppose you are going to a restaurant that you've never been to before? What does the entrance look like? Is there a parking lot on that block? Is there a place to lock up your bike? Street view can help you determine these things.

Getting Traffic Reports

Although Satellite views and Street view give you old photos, there is a way to get up-to-the minute data on your maps. For major cities, you can even get traffic information on your maps.

1. Bring up a Map view that shows some highways and major boulevards.

2. Tap the page corner.

3. Turn on Traffic overlays.

4. The map now shows green, yellow, and red indicators along highways and major streets representing fast-to-slow traffic patterns.

Search Apple's App Store for thousands of useful, educational, and entertaining apps.

To go beyond the basic functionality of your iPad, you need to learn how to add more apps using the App Store.

→ Purchasing an App

→ Arranging Apps on Your iPad

→ Arranging Apps Using iTunes

→ Creating App Folders

→ Viewing Currently Running Apps

→ Finding Good Apps

→ Using iPhone/iPod touch Apps

→ Getting Help with Apps

→ Telling Friends About Apps

The World of Apps

Apps that come with your iPad and the iWork suite are just the tip of the iceberg. The App Store contains thousands of apps from third-party developers, with more added each day.

You use the App Store app to shop for and purchase new apps—although many are free. You can also rearrange the app icons on your Home screen pages to organize them.

Purchasing an App

Adding a new app to your iPad requires that you visit the App Store. You do that, not surprisingly, with the App Store app on your Home screen.

1. Tap the App Store icon on your Home screen.

2. You see the featured apps at the top of the screen.

3. Tap the left and right arrows in the New and Noteworthy section to see more apps.

4. Scroll down to see more apps, such as Staff Favorites.

5. Tap What's Hot to switch to Featured, What's Hot or tap All for a sortable list of apps.

6. Tap Top Charts to see the top paid apps and top free apps.

7. Tap Categories to see a list of app categories.

8. Tap any category to go to the page of featured apps in that category.

9. Tap the filter buttons at the top of the screen to further define what you are looking for.

10. Tap the Sort By button to sort by Popularity, Release Date, or Rating.

11. Tap an app to read more about it.

And Sometimes Someone Buys You Lunch

If you go to the bottom of any listings page in the App Store, you will see a button marked Redeem. Use this to enter any redemption code you get for a free app. You may get a code because someone sends you an app as a gift. Developers also send out a handful of these codes when they release a new app or app version.

12. The app's page displays screen-shots, other apps by the same company, and user reviews.

13. Tap on the price on the left under the large icon to purchase an app. It changes to a Buy App button. Tap it again. If you have already purchased the app, the button will simply say "Installed."

14. The app starts installing, and you can watch the progress from your Home screen.

Arranging Apps on Your iPad

It doesn't take long to have several pages of apps. Fortunately, you can rearrange your app icons in two ways. The first is to do it on the iPad.

1. Tap and hold an icon until all the icons start to jiggle.

2. The icon you are holding is a little larger than the others. Drag it and drop it in a new location. To carry the icon to the next page of apps, drag it to the right side of the screen.

3. Delete an app from your iPad by tapping the X at the upper left of the icon.

Deleting Is Not Forever

If you sync your iPad to iTunes on a computer, you do not delete apps forever. All apps remain in your iTunes library on your computer unless you remove them. So you can get rid of the app from your iPad and find it is still on your computer if you want to select it to sync back to your iPad.

4. To stop the jiggling, press the Home button.

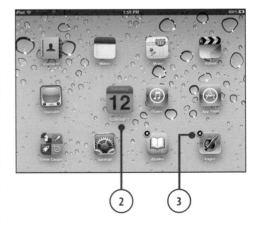

>>> Go Further

WHAT ELSE CAN I DO?

Here are a few more tips that might make your app housekeeping easier:

- You can release an app and then grab another to move it. If the apps still jiggle, you can keep moving app icons.

- You can drag apps into the dock along the bottom where you can fit up to six apps. Apps in the dock appear on all pages of your Home screen.

- You can drag an app to the right on the last page of apps to create a new page of your Home screen.

Arranging Apps Using iTunes

A better way to arrange your apps is to use iTunes. You can not only move the apps around on the pages, but you can also clearly see which ones get synced to your iPad and which ones are merely archives on your computer.

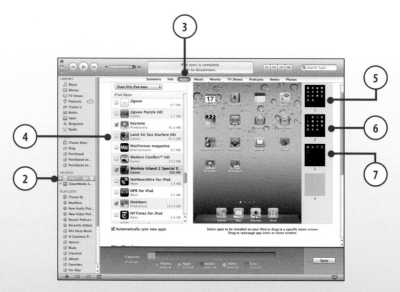

1. Connect your iPad to your computer and launch iTunes.

2. Select your iPad in the left sidebar.

3. Choose the Apps button on the right to see a representation of your iPad Home screen. On the far right you can see each page of the Home screen. On the left is an alphabetical list of apps you have on your computer. If a check mark is next to the app, that app is set to sync to your iPad.

   Following are some of the things you can do to rearrange your apps:

   - Click the pages to the right to jump around to the different pages of your Home screen.

   - Double-click the app on the left to jump to the page where the app is located.

   - Click and drag an app around on a page just like you would on your iPad.

   - Drag an app to a page in the list on the right to move it to another page.

   - Hold down the shift key and click multiple apps. You can then drag the whole selection to another page.

4. From the list on the left, uncheck any items that you don't want on your iPad.

Use Sort and Search

If you have a lot of apps, it might be easier to sort them by category or date. You can use the pop-up menu at the top of the left column for that. You can also type in the search field. You don't need to type a complete name. You can also use terms like "game" or "news" to search for apps and narrow down the list a bit.

5. Go to page 1 of your apps and move any apps off of the page that aren't the default iPad apps that came with your iPad. Move them to page 3.

6. Go to page 2 of your apps and move everything except iBooks, the iWork apps, and your most critical use-all-the-time apps.

7. Starting with page 3, create sets of apps on each page that match a theme: communications, games, photography, and so on.

   These last three steps are just a suggestion. You can arrange things differently.

Creating App Folders

In addition to spreading your apps across multiple pages, you can also group them together in folders so that several apps take up only one icon position on a screen.

1. Identify several apps on the same screen that you want to group together. Tap and hold one of those apps until the icons start to jiggle.

2. Continue to hold your finger down, and drag the icon to another one you wish to group it with.

3. An app folder appears, and all other app icons should fade so you can focus on your new app folder.

4. Change the name of the app folder.

5. Press the Home button once to dismiss the name editor, and again to return to your home screen.

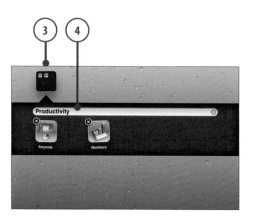

6. You now see the app folder on your home screen. You can drag other apps to this folder using steps 1 and 2.

   After you have created an app folder, you can access the apps in it by first tapping on the folder and then tapping the app you want to launch. Tapping and holding any app in the folder gives you the opportunity to rename the folder, rearrange the icons in the folder, or drag an app out of the folder.

Viewing Currently Running Apps

You can have many apps running at once on your iPad. In fact, after you launch an app it will remain running by default even if you switch back to the home screen and run another app. Apps running in the background use little or no resources. You can think of them as paused apps. You can switch back to them at any time, and most apps will resume right where you left off.

1. Double-press the Home button. This brings up the list of recent apps at the bottom of the screen.

2. You can flick back and forth to view apps further down the list.

3. Tap an app to return to it.

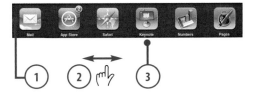

4. Press the Home button to simply exit the list.

5. If you flick to the right, you will get to a special part of the list that includes controls for the app you are currently using.

Quitting Apps

Although it is rarely necessary to completely quit an app, you can do it here in the list of recent apps. Just tap and hold any app icon. They will all start to jiggle, and a red minus button will appear with each one. Tap that button to stop that app from running. If you were in the middle of something, like a game or a document, you may lose that data. You can then press the Home button to return to the home screen and launch the app again.

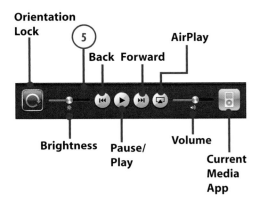

Finding Good Apps

Finding good apps might be the biggest problem that iPad users have. With more than 140,000 apps in the App Store, it can be hard to find what you want, so here are some tips.

1. Check out the featured apps in the App Store, but be wary because they tend to be heavy on apps by large companies with well-established brands.

2. In iTunes on your computer, find an app close to what you want and then check out the Customers Also Bought section.

3. Look for trial versions, which often have names with "Lite" or "Free" at the end. Search for the name of the app and see if other versions turn up.

4. Read reviews, but don't trust them completely. Casual users are not always the best at providing balanced reviews.

USING RESOURCES OUTSIDE THE APP STORE

Many good resources for finding apps aren't part of the App Store. Following are a few suggestions:

- Search using Google. For example, if you want another spreadsheet app, search "iPad App Spreadsheet."

- After you find an app that you want, try another Google search using the name of the app followed by the word "review."

- Find sites that feature and review apps. Many are out there, but be aware that some sites are paid by developers to review an app, so the review might not be the most objective.

- The author provides a list of recommended apps at http://macmost.com/featurediphoneapps.

Using iPhone/iPod touch Apps

One of the great things about using apps on the iPad is that you can use almost every app in Apple's App Store—including those originally made for the iPhone and iPod Touch.

Four types of apps are in the store from an iPad-owner's perspective. A few are iPhone/iPod Touch only. Avoid those, naturally. The majority are iPhone/iPod Touch apps that also work on the iPad. These apps appear in the middle of the screen or scale to double the size. Some might work better than others on the iPad.

You can also find apps that work only on the iPad, which are listed in the App Store separately from the iPhone apps.

There are apps that work on the iPhone, but on the iPad they scale up to full reso-lution and work just like an iPad-only app. These apps are listed on both the iPhone and iPad sides of the App Store.

1. To enlarge the app, tap the 2x button at the lower-right corner.

2. If the app looks blurry when it's enlarged, tap the 1x button to return to normal size.

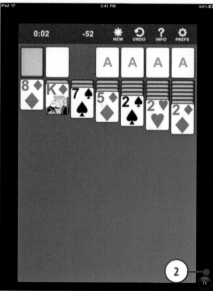

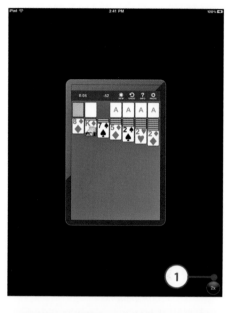

Getting Help with Apps

Apps are developed rapidly by both large and small companies. And apps are difficult to test because of Apple's restrictions on app distribution. So it is common to find bugs, have problems, or simply need to ask a question.

1. Check in the app to see if you can contact the developer. For example, in the USA Today app, an i button brings up a window for providing feedback.

2. Tap Email Support? button (or a similar button in another app) to email the developer right from the app.

3. If you don't find a way to contact support in the app, launch the App Store app and search for the app there.

4. On the left you usually see links to both the developer's website and App Support. Try the website first to see if there is a forum, documentation, or even a FAQ.

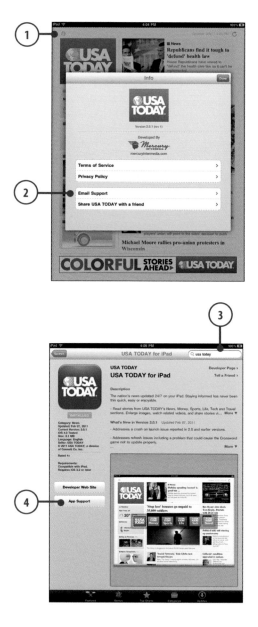

Telling Friends About Apps

If you find an app you like, tell your friends about it. Word of mouth is one of the primary ways that good apps rise to the top.

1. In the App Store app, search and find the app you want to talk about.

2. Tap Tell a Friend.

3. A new email message opens, with the subject and body all filled out. It even adds a large app icon.

4. Using iTunes on your computer, you can click the Menu button next to the Buy App button to bring up a pop-up window, and then tap Tell a Friend in the pop-up window.

5. Copy the link to include in an email or blog post.

6. Share it on Facebook or Twitter.

7. Purchase a copy of the app as a gift for a friend.

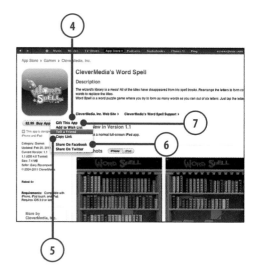

Family Sharing

When you buy an app, it can be put on any iPad (or iPhone/iPod touch if it works there, too) registered to your iTunes account? So if you share an iTunes account with your entire family, you can share your apps as well. No need to buy them again for a second iPad.

Create and maintain
databases.

View and control your
desktop computer.

Store and view
documents.

Read RSS
and news
feeds.

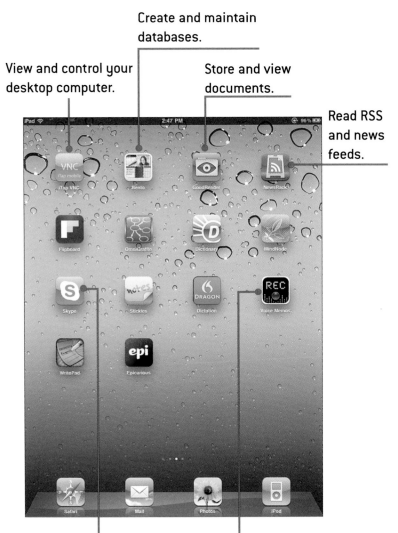

Make phone calls
using your iPad.

Record voice
reminderss.

In this chapter, we take a look at various apps that you should add to your iPad to make it even more useful.

→ Using iTap VNC

→ Using Bento

→ Using GoodReader

→ Using NewsRack

→ Using Flipboard

→ Using OmniGraffle

→ Adding a Dictionary and Thesaurus

→ Using MindNode

→ Using Skype

→ Putting Notes on Your Home/Lock Screen

→ Talking to Your iPad

→ Recording Voice Memos

→ Handwriting Notes

→ Using Epicurious

→ Other Useful Apps

Using Popular and Critical Apps

Ask almost anyone what the best feature of the iPad is and you'll get the same answer: all the apps! The App Store is not only a source of hundreds of thousands of useful, interesting, and fun apps, but it grows each day as third-party developers and Apple add more. Here's a look at how to use some of the most popular apps for the iPad to perform various useful tasks.

Using iTap VNC

Your iPad can be a window to your Mac or PC. By using Virtual Network Computing (VNC) technology, you can control your computer just like it was sitting in front of you (except you can't hear the sound output).

1. Search in the App Store for iTap VNC and download it. Tap the icon to launch the app.

2. On the screen that shows your current bookmarks, tap Add Manual Bookmark.

3. Enter the IP address of your computer under Host.

4. Tap Credentials and enter your ID and password for VNC access to that computer.

5. Tap Save.

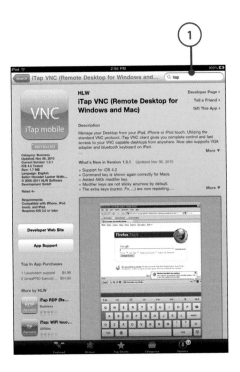

Setting Up VNC on Your Computer

It takes two to VNC. You need to set up your Mac or Windows computer to accept the connection and allow your iPad to take over the screen. On a Mac, you can do this by turning on Screen Sharing in the Sharing pane of System Preferences. On Windows, it is called Remote Desktop, or you can install a third-party VNC server.

Other VNC Apps

There are many other VNC apps like iTap VNC. Also check out iTeleport for iPad, Desktop Connect, and LogMeIn Ignition. A slightly different app to look at is Air Display. It lets you use your iPad as an extra screen with your Mac.

6. After initial setup, the next time you use iTap VNC, you are prompted to select the computer from a bookmark list. Tap the name of the bookmark to establish a connection.

7. After you are connected, you will see a portion of your computer's screen.

Why Won't It Work?

Getting VNC connections to work can be frustrating. It has nothing to do with the iPad. Getting them to work between a laptop and a desktop has the same difficulties. If your network router or Internet modem isn't set up just right, it won't connect and you have little indication as to why. Most of the time, VNC connections work right away, but if you are one of the unlucky few, you might need to tinker around with your network equipment settings or even call in an expert to get it to work.

8. Tap and drag to move around to see your whole screen.

9. Pinch to zoom in and out.

10. To type into an application from a keyboard, first select the application to type in by tapping, as you would click it on your computer.

11. Swipe down with three fingers on your iPad screen to open the keyboard.

12. Dismiss the keyboard with the button at the lower-right corner.

Using Bento

When you want to keep track of more than just contacts and events on your iPad, you can use Bento for iPad to create and maintain a database on your iPad. You can even sync it to your Mac if you have Bento for Mac.

1. Search for Bento in the App Store, install it, and then tap its icon on the Home screen.

2. If this is your first time using Bento, you will see a welcome screen. Tap the Start using Bento button. Otherwise, tap the Libraries button.

3. Tap the + button to add a new library.

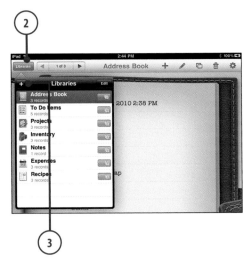

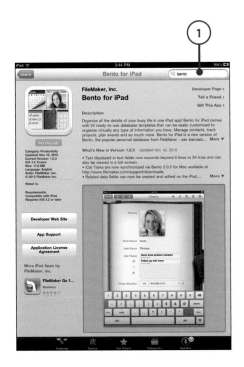

4. Flip through the kinds of libraries available. For this example, we start with a blank library.

5. Tap the Create Library button.

6. To add a field, tap the Pencil button.

7. Tap the New Field element (the + symbol) and drag it down to the page to add a new field.

8. Change the selection to Text if it isn't already selected.

9. Tap Create.

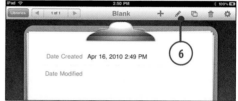

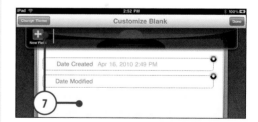

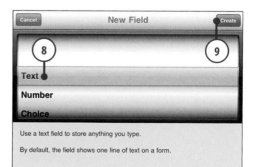

10. Enter a name for the field.

11. Tap Create.

12. Drag a new field on to the page again, but this time select Choice as the type of field.

Lots of Field Types

Bento includes all the standard field types, such as numbers, check boxes, time, date, and so on. You can even have an image field and link it to something in your Photos albums.

---

13. Tap Create.

14. Enter a name for this field.

15. Tap Add a New Choice and enter the choice name of Movie.

16. Add another choice and name it TV Show and then add a third choice of Home Video.

17. Tap Create.

18. Tap Done.

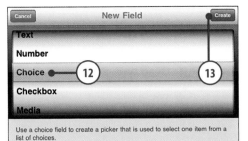

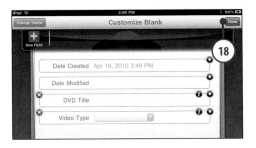

19. Tap next to the first field you created to enter data.

20. Tap next to the second field to select a choice.

21. Tap the + button to add another record to the database. Repeat steps 19 to 21 to enter more data.

Using GoodReader

While iBooks is great for basic document viewing, those more serious about collecting documents to read on their iPad have looked to apps that have even more features. Apps such as GoodReader enable you to create a library of viewable files such as PDFs, Word, images, text, and so on. You can then access these documents any time.

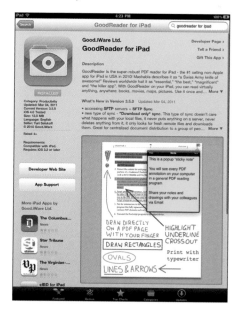

1. Search the App Store for GoodReader and add it to your apps. On your Mac or PC, with your iPad connected, select it on the left in iTunes.

2. Select the Apps button.

3. At the bottom of the Apps page, select GoodReader.

4. Drag and drop PDF and other files into the GoodReader Documents folder. That document is instantly synced with your iPad.

5. Run the GoodReader app on your iPad.

6. On the left side, double-tap on the name of the document to read it.

When you view a PDF file, you can pinch to zoom in and out. You can also tap different parts of the screen to move around in the document. Tapping the center of the screen will bring up buttons at the top and bottom.

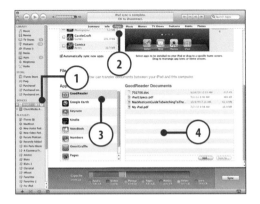

7. Tap in the center of the screen to bring up buttons at top and bottom and a scroll bar on the left side.

8. Tap in the center near the bottom to go to the next page.

9. Tap on the right side of the screen to go to the next page.

Using NewsRack

If you read a lot of online news and blogs, you probably use RSS from time to time to view these sources as feeds, rather than visiting the website. NewsRack is one RSS feed reader for the iPad.

1. Search the App Store for NewsRack and add it to your apps. After it has been installed, launch NewsRack.

2. Tap Add Feeds. (Or use Sync Settings to sync your Google Reader settings.)

3. Tap the Add Feed button. This will look very different in horizontal screen orientation, so keep it vertical for now.

4. In the Enter Feed URL field, enter the domain name for a website.

5. Tap Show Feeds. A list of RSS feeds from the site will appear.

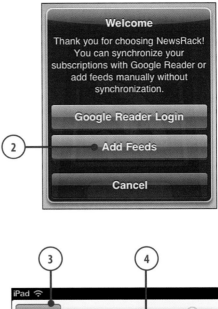

Finding RSS Feeds

RSS feeds are everywhere. Chances are your local newspaper and your favorite blogs and online magazines all have RSS feeds. Try the URL for any website in NewsRack and see what feeds are available.

6. Tap the + button to the left of any feed you want to subscribe to.

7. Tap the back menu button (labeled Add Feed on this example) until you get a Done button, so you can complete the action of adding feeds.

Lots of RSS Reader Apps

Since the iPad is an ideal device for reading the news, many RSS reader apps have appeared. Other popular ones include Pulse News Reader, NetNewsWire, GoReader Pro and Reeder for iPad. Search in the App Store for "rss reader," and you will come up with even more.

8. Tap Feeds at the top to look at a list of all your RSS feeds.

9. Tap Unread to view all the unread items in all your feeds. Alternatively, tap a single feed to just see that feed.

10. You see a mix of all the unread items in all your feeds. Tap any one to read it.

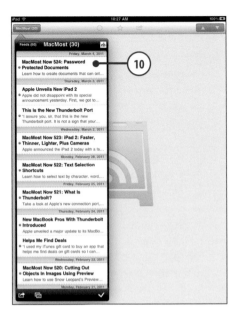

>>> Go Further

MAKE THE iPAD YOUR NEW NEWSPAPER

No need to get a physical paper dropped on your doorstep anymore. Many major newspapers and magazines deliver via their iPad apps. Look for apps from *USA Today*, the *New York Times*, the *Wall Street Journal*, *Newsweek*, *Time*, and *Wired*. There is even an iPad-only newspaper called *The Daily*. You can even create your own newspaper using multiple sources with the app The Early Edition.

In some cases the app and the daily content are free. Sometimes you need to pay for the app, but the content is free. Other times, such as with magazines, you pay for each issue you download. For newspapers like *The Daily*, you can sign up for a weekly subscription fee.

Newspapers that don't have a custom app can still be viewed in the iPad's web browser, often with more up-to-date content than you can get with a paper edition.

Using Flipboard

How about a newspaper that is all about you? Well, at least about your friends and things that you like. Such a thing exists, and it is called Flipboard. It uses information from your Facebook and Twitter accounts to show pictures and posts from your friends. Then it uses your RSS feeds to show you news you are interested in. To see page after page of things that should interest you, just keep flipping.

1. Search for Flipboard in the App Store. Then install it and launch it.

2. Tap to enter your Twitter login information.

3. Tap to enter your Facebook login information.

4. Tap to create a new content section.

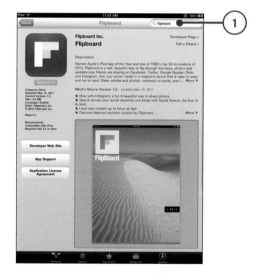

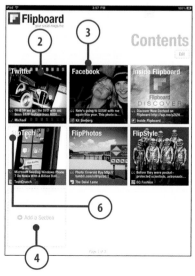

5. You can add RSS feeds or your entire Google Reader account.

6. Tap a section to jump to it.

7. Flip by swiping right to left to turn the page. Each page shows a different layout with content from that section's source.

8. Share things you like on Twitter and Facebook.

Using OmniGraffle

If you ever need to create charts or diagrams on your iPad, OmniGraffle is for you. Search the App Store for OmniGraffle and add the app.

1. Search for and install OmniGraffle from the App Store, and then launch it.

2. You may see the demonstration diagram when you first launch OmniGraffle. If so, tap the Diagrams button at the upper left, and then tap New Diagram.

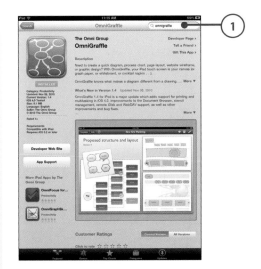

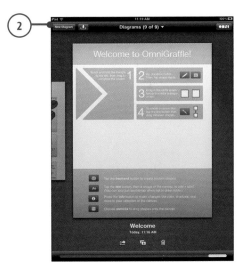

3. Tap the Stencils button.

4. Tap Shapes.

5. Tap the rounded rectangle and drag it to the empty space.

6. Tap and drag the bottom-right corner of the new rectangle, and stretch it to make it larger.

7. Double-tap in the middle to enter some text. Repeat steps 3 through 7 to create several other rectangles on the organization chart.

8. Tap the Pencil tool.

9. Tap the top rectangle and hold until it gets a green outline. Drag to one of the other rectangles and release.

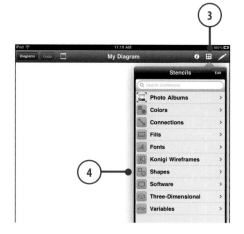

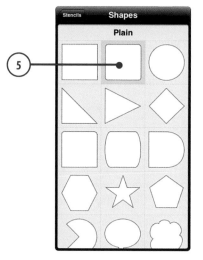

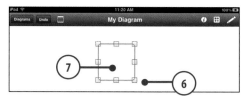

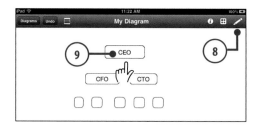

10. A line from one box to the other forms. Repeat this step to create the other connections.

11. Tap Done.

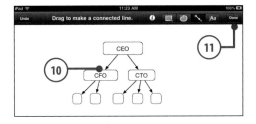

Adding a Dictionary and Thesaurus

It would be a crime to have to carry a dictionary with you in addition to your iPad. Of course, the solution is to get a Dictionary app for your iPad. The Dictionary.com app is a free download from the App Store.

1. Find the Dictionary.com app in the App Store, install it, and then launch it.

Use Any Online Dictionary

Of course if you prefer another dictionary that doesn't have an iPad app, you can always just bookmark that site in Safari. You can also create a Home screen bookmark as we did in Chapter 7, "Surfing the Web."

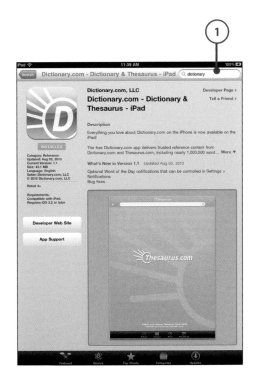

2. Tap in the search box and enter a word to look up.

3. A list of suggestions appears. Or you can just tap Search in the on-screen keyboard.

4. You can even tap the Speaker icon in many cases and hear a pronunciation.

5. Tap Thesaurus at the bottom to switch to using the thesaurus.

6. Tap on any of the words in the lists to jump to the thesaurus entry for that word.

7. While moving from word to word in the thesaurus, you can always tap Dictionary again to get a definition for the current word.

Using MindNode

Another type of organizational software program is called mind mapping. Mind maps look like organizational charts, but each box represents a thought or idea. MindNode for iPad is a mind-mapping program.

1. Search for MindNode in the App Store, install it, and then launch it from your home screen.

2. The first time you run MindNode, you start with a blank mind map. Inside, you start off with a single node or box. Double-tap on this Mind Map node to name it.

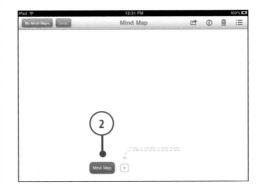

3. Type a name for the main node of the mind map.

4. Tap Done.

5. Drag the + box out from the main node to create a new node.

6. Name the new node.

7. Repeat steps 5 and 6 to add new nodes.

8. Tap Done.

9. Your completed mind map can have as many nodes and sub-nodes as you need.

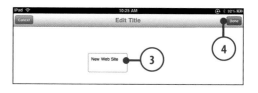

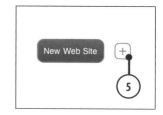

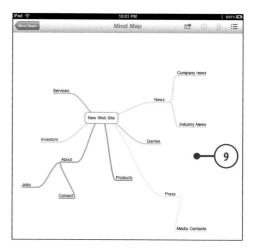

Using Skype

Your iPad works quite well as a phone when you use a VoIP (voice over IP) app. Skype is probably the most well known.

1. Search for Skype in the App Store. It won't show up under iPad apps, as it is an iPhone app. Install it and then launch it.

It's Not an iPad App!

At the time of this writing, the Skype app is formatted for iPhone only but works just fine on the iPad. You can use it in native 1x screen mode, or tap the 2x button to enlarge the app on your screen. Perhaps by the time you read this, the app will work on the iPad in full-screen mode.

2. When you run the Skype app, you need to enter your ID and password and then sign in. After you do this the first time, you can skip this screen.

Get a Skype Account

You need a Skype account to use the Skype app. You can get a free one at http://www.skype.com/. If you find the service useful, you might want to upgrade to a paid account, which lets you call land lines and other phones. The free account lets you call only other Skype users.

3. Use the on-screen keypad to enter a phone number. You need a country code, too, which means using a 1 for U.S. calls. It should be there by default.

4. Tap Call.

5. While making a call, you see the elapsed time, and Mute and Hold buttons. Use the Dialpad button when you need to dial numbers during a call.

6. Tap End Call to hang up.

How Do You Hold Your iPad to Talk?

The microphone is at the top of your iPad 2. The speaker is at the bottom on the back. The best way may be to just put the iPad in front of you and ignore the locations of both. Or, you can get a set of iPhone earbuds.

How About Skype Video?

You can also make video calls with Skype using your iPad 2's cameras. The quality isn't great, but because the app is formatted for an iPhone screen rather than an iPad screen, it at least does work. Hopefully the Skype app will be updated soon to look better on the iPad.

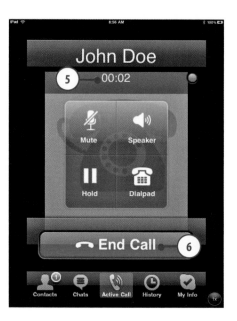

Putting Notes on Your Home/Lock Screen

Your Lock screen and Home screen backgrounds look pretty. But can they be functional? One app attempts to make them more useful by enabling you to put sticky notes on them. Search in the App Store for Stick It and add it to your collection of apps.

1. Search for Sticky Notes HD in the App Store. Install it and then launch it.

2. Tap + to create a new note. You may be asked to choose Small or Large. Choose Large.

3. Select a color from the list. You can also select different note types, such as talk bubbles, pieces of paper, or even just plain text boxes.

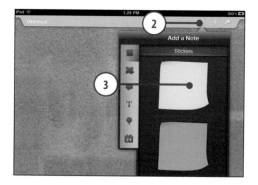

4. Type a note using the on-screen keyboard.

5. Tap Done.

6. Drag the note into a better position.

7. Tap the bottom-left corner to pick a background image.

8. Choose a background from the Library, Colors, or Photos buttons. Tap a new background.

9. Tap Done.

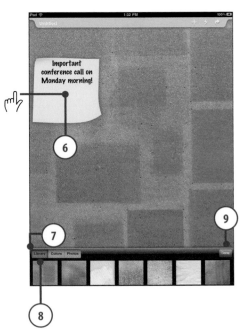

10. Tap the Export button.

11. Tap Save to Camera Roll.

12. Tap Dismiss.

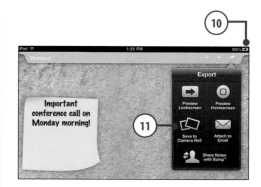

The App Can't Do It for You

Although the Stick It app is great for making backgrounds with notes on them, it can't make these backgrounds your Lock or Home screen. You have to do that yourself using the Photos app or the Brightness & Wallpaper settings in the Settings app.

13. Press your Home button to return to the Home screen and then tap the Photos icon.

14. Find the photo you just took and tap it.

15. Tap the Boxed Arrow button.

16. Tap Use as Wallpaper.

17. Tap Set Lock Screen.

18. Press the Wake/Sleep Button at the top of your iPad.

19. Press the Home button.

20. The background, complete with the sticky note, now appears on your Lock screen.

Emergency Contact Info

Another use for this app is to quickly and easily put your emergency contact information on the Lock screen. You can just put a "In case of emergency" phone number and instructions on the screen, or "If found, please call:" phone number.

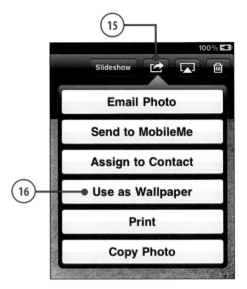

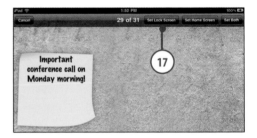

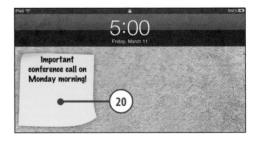

Talking to Your iPad

Because your iPad has a microphone, and a powerful processor, it is well suited for taking dictation. The Dragon Dictation app types what you speak into the iPad.

1. Search for Dragon Dictation in the App Store, install it, and launch it. You may have to set your location and agree to the user agreement the first time you run it.

2. Tap the button in the middle of the screen and start speaking clearly at a normal pace.

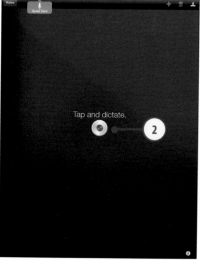

3. Tap in the middle of the screen when done.

4. After a short delay, the text appears on the screen.

5. Tap the Keyboard button at the bottom of the screen to bring up the on-screen keyboard and make corrections.

6. Tap the Arrow button at the top-right part to copy the text to the clipboard so you can use it elsewhere, or send it via email.

7. Tap the button at the top to record some more.

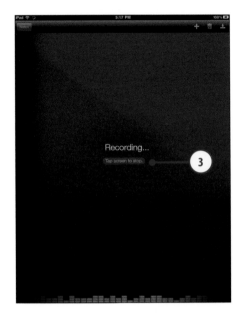

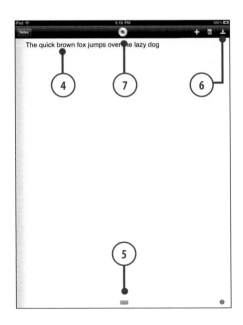

It's Not All Good

ACCURACY?

So you want your iPad to listen to you and transcribe what you say perfectly? This isn't *Star Trek*. There are going to be mistakes. After a while you learn how to minimize errors by changing the way you dictate to the app, but you always need to carefully edit your text when you finish recording.

Recording Voice Memos

The dictation is nice, but what if you just want to record some notes to yourself? The Voice Memos app enables you to record yourself, or anything, and save it. You can then play the recording back or email it.

1. Find the "Voice Memos for iPad" app in the App Store. Install it and launch it.

2. Tap the Record button to start recording and speak your message.

3. Tap the Stop button to stop recording.

4. Tap the Voice Memos button at the top-left corner to see a list of memos you have recorded.

5. Tap a memo to play it back.

6. Tap the blue button to change the name of the memo.

7. After selecting a memo and playing it, tap the Email button to send it via email.

8. Tap the Delete button to remove the recording.

You Want Audio While Taking Notes?

If you want to record audio and take notes at the same time, try the app SoundNote. You can tap out text with the keyboard and draw with your finger all while audio is being recorded. Then it remembers where the audio stream was for each word. So tap a word to hear the audio at that moment. Wish I had this back in college!

Handwriting Notes

You'd think with a touch screen that the iPad could recognize your handwriting instead of making you type on an on-screen keyboard. The WritePad app enables you to take notes by typing or by using the touch screen to write with your finger.

1. Find WritePad in the App Store. Install it and launch it.

2. Tap the My Documents button to view your current documents.

3. Tap + to start a new document.

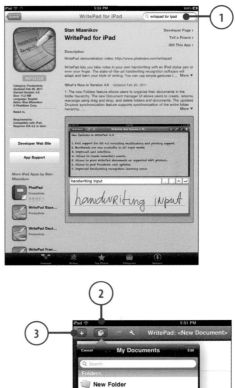

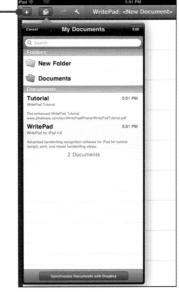

4. Tap and drag around the screen using the tip of your finger like a pen or pencil. Start in the upper-left corner. You can use printed letters, cursive, or a mixture.

5. Stop writing and wait for the text to process. When it does, the text appears at the cursor location.

6. Tap the buttons at the top-right corner to switch between Reading mode, Writing mode, and Keyboard mode.

7. Tap the Undo button to undo the last text processed.

Looking for a Different Handwriting App?

If you'd rather have an excellent app that just lets you write and draw on the screen, try Penultimate. You create notebooks and write in them by drawing with your finger. You can also mark up PDF documents and enter text using the on-screen keyboard.

Using Epicurious

One application for early personal computers was to store and recall recipes. With the Internet, we can also share those recipes. And now with the iPad, there is finally a way to easily have these recipes with you in the kitchen while cooking. The Epicurious app is a favorite for such tasks.

1. Search for Epicurious in the App Store. Download and launch.

2. Tap the Control Panel to see a list of featured sections.

3. Use the search box to search for a recipe.

4. Tap a section.

5. Tap a recipe.

6. You'll get a list of ingredients needed.

7. You can then follow the recipe. If only cooking were that easy! Bon Appetit!

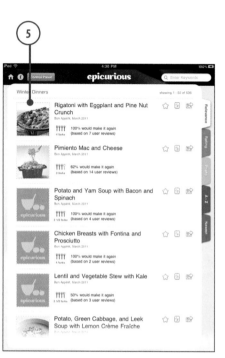

Other Useful Apps

So many useful apps are in the store that it is impossible to cover them all in a book. Here are some quick mentions of others you can check out. Some are free, others you have to pay for.

- **SketchBook Pro**: This drawing app lets you paint with your fingers. Professional artists have used it to create some amazing pieces. There is even a Flickr gallery of SketchBook pro art. You should also check out **Brushes**, **ArtStudio**, and the free **Adobe Ideas** app.

- **1Password**: Mac users already know about the popular 1Password for Mac. The iPad version doesn't integrate with Safari, but it does give you a place to securely store passwords and other important information.

- **Twitter**: The official Twitter app for iPad is more than just a simple Twitter viewer. Clever ways in which the windows overlay themselves allow you to quickly and easily check out what is going on in your Twitter world and keep your followers updated. Also, while it is really an iPhone app, the free official **Facebook** app is a must-have for Facebook users.

- **Things**: If you are into productivity apps and to-do lists, check out Things. It is the king of to-do list apps on the iPad. Also check out **Toodledo** and **2Do**.

- **Evernote**: The great thing about the popular Evernote app is not that you can take notes, record audio, and take pictures, but that these all sync to your online account. So if you take a note on your iPad, it will appear in Evernote on your iPhone, Mac, or PC.

- **StarWalk**: This is a must-have app for anyone even vaguely interested in astronomy. Even if you aren't, the beautiful, up-to-the-minute renderings of the night sky on your iPad will impress your friends. You can see what the sky looks like right now, right where you are, and use it as a guide to identifying what you see. Also check out **The Elements: A Visual Exploration** for more cool science learning.

- **Wolfram Alpha**: Want to compare two stocks, see the molecular structure of sulfuric acid, or calculate the amount of sodium in your breakfast? Would you believe that one app does all three and has hundreds of other interesting answers to all sorts of questions.

- **USA Today**: While other national newspapers are playing around with pay-to-read models, *USA Today* is sticking with free. It provides a great summary of what is going on around the country. If you are looking for a more European perspective, the **BBC News** app also provides news, plus a lot of video.

- **Zinio**: While some magazines have their own apps, many others can be found inside Zinio. It is like having a magazine stand inside your iPad. Browse sample articles for free and then look for magazines you can purchase either as a single issue or a subscription. You can even get European and Asian magazines that are hard to find in the U.S.

- **The Weather Channel Max+**: If you get your news on your iPad, you might as well get the weather, too. This free app covers it all, with maps, forecasts, current conditions, and even video. But there are plenty of other weather apps in the store, too. Check out **Weather HD** in particular.

Read comics.

Listen to music.

Stream movies and TV shows.

Play games.

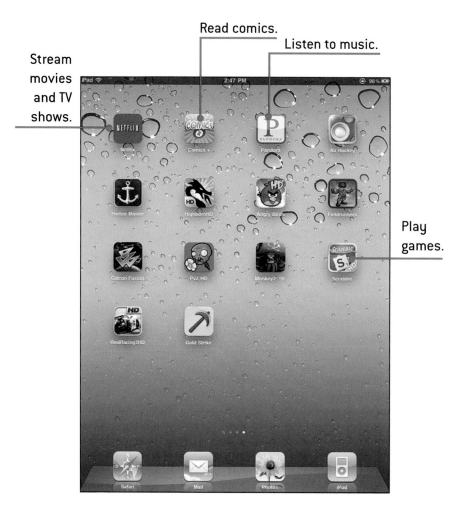

In this chapter, we look at apps that exist for entertainment purposes such as viewing movies, reading comics, listening to music, or playing games.

→ Composing Music with GarageBand

→ Watching Movies and TV Shows with Netflix

→ Reading Comics

→ Listening to Music with Pandora Radio

→ Using Game Center

→ Playing iPad Games

Games and Entertainment

You can view a lot of information and get a lot of work done on the iPad, but it is still a great device for entertainment. The majority of entertainment apps out there are games, but there are also some general entertainment apps that we can take a look at.

Composing Music with GarageBand

It is hard to sum up GarageBand in just a few pages. This little brother to the Mac GarageBand application is a very big app. It could almost deserve a book all to itself. Let's look at how to create a simple song.

1. Find GarageBand in the App Store. Install it and launch it from the home screen.

2. Tap the + button and then New Song.

3. Now you can choose an instrument to start. Select the keyboard.

4. Tap the keys to play notes. The force at which you hit the keys and the spot on the key determines the exact sound it produces.

5. Tap the instrument button to change from Grand Piano to one of dozens of other instruments.

6. Tap the record button to record what you are playing. A metronome will count down, so wait one measure before starting. Try just a few notes, only one or two measures.

7. Tap the Stop button when you are done recording.

8. Tap the Undo button if you didn't quite get the notes right. Then try again.

9. After you have recorded a bit of music, the View button will appear. You can use that to switch to the Tracks view.

10. In Tracks view you will see the bit of music you recorded. Tap on it once to select it. Tap again to bring up a menu that includes Cut, Copy, Delete, Loop, and Split. Tap Loop.

11. The music you recorded is now set to loop for the entire section of the song. Tap the Play button to test it.

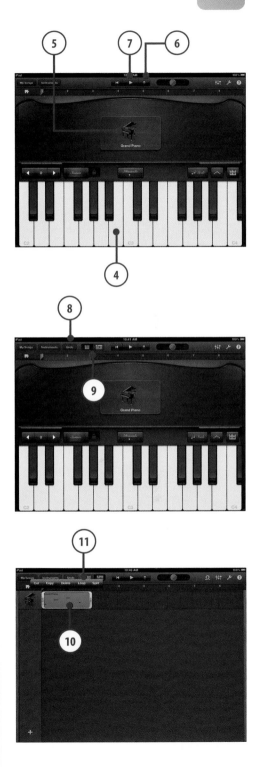

12. Tap the Loop button to view pre-made loops that you can add to your song.

13. You can filter the list of loops by Instrument, Genre, or keywords.

14. Select a loop to test it. You can even have your loop playing at the same time by tapping the Play button at the top and then tap-ping a loop from the Apple Loops menu to see how they sound together.

15. Drag a loop from the list to the area right under the loop you cre-ated.

16. Now you have your original loop and a drum loop. Tap play to hear them together.

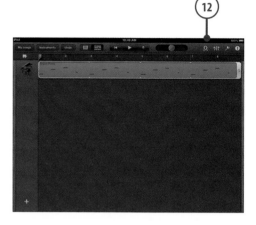

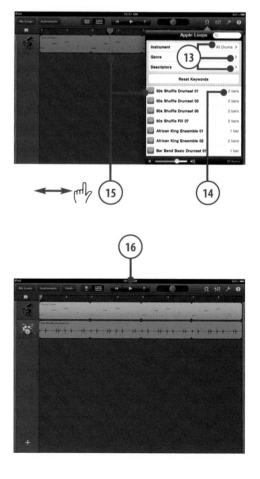

You can now continue to add loops. Add a bass line and maybe some gui-tar. You can also double-tap on the left side of each track where you see the image of the instrument, to return to the instrument view and switch instruments or record more notes.

Besides the piano, you can also play guitar, bass, or drums. And each instrument has several variations. Plus, there are smart instruments, such as the smart guitar that only allows you to play notes and chords that fit well together.

See http://macmost.com/ipadguide/ for more tutorials on using GarageBand for iPad.

Watching Movies and TV Shows with Netflix

Netflix started as a DVD rental service using mail rather than retail stores, but it is quickly changing into an online video rental service. One of the first acclaimed apps for the iPad was the Netflix app. Netflix subscribers can use it to rent and watch movies right on their iPads.

1. Enter your email address and password, and then tap Sign In. If you don't have an account, you can actually sign up for a trial account right on your iPad.

2. Tap an image to start streaming the video.

3. Tap the information next to an image to find out more about the video.

4. In this case, the video is actually a TV series, so another screen appears with a list of episodes. Tap an episode to watch it.

5. The movie should start after a few seconds. You have Play and Pause controls at the bottom of the screen.

What Happened to the Controls?

The controls around the movie disappear after a few seconds of viewing. You can always bring them back by tapping the center of the screen.

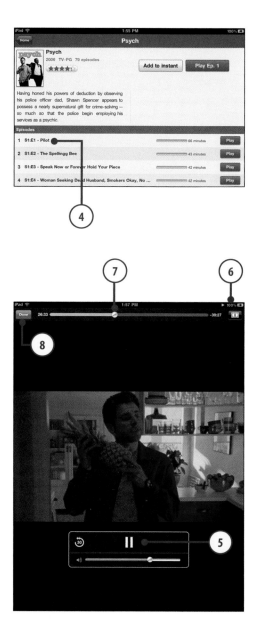

6. You can tap the Zoom button at the upper-right corner to zoom in slightly to the center of the screen.

7. Use the large slider at the top to jump around in the movie.

8. Tap the Done button to return to the previous screen.

You Have to Be Online

Although watching movies in the Netflix app is unlimited, you can't download and store the movie for later viewing. You need to be online to watch. iTunes rentals, on the other hand, can be stored and watched while offline, like on an airplane flight.

Reading Comics

The iPad is a great platform for reading comics. The Comics + app is one of the many comic book apps that enables you to purchase and read comics. It has some of the best graphic quality and you can even download some free comics to try it out.

1. Browse either paid or free comics.

2. Browse through the offerings.

3. Search for a comic.

4. Tap the price button next to any comic to download it. The price will simply read FREE if the comic doesn't cost anything.

5. Tap My Comics at the bottom to see the comics in your iPad collection.

6. Tap the Read button next to a comic to open it.

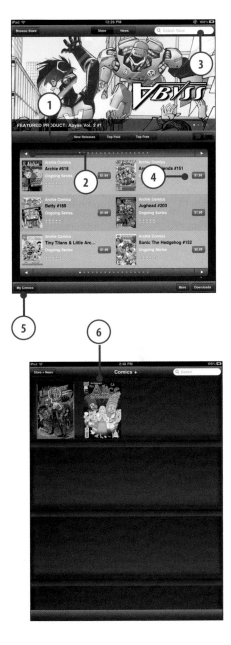

7. Tap in the screen to bring up a toolbar at the top and a scan bar at the bottom.

8. Flick right to left to turn the page.

9. Tap done to return to the list of your comics.

Plenty of Comics

There are dozens of quality comics in the App Store. Some comics even have their own app. Look for the Marvel Comics app, the Comics app, DC Comics, IDW Comics, Comic Zeal, and others. Most apps that allow you to download various issues are free and charge you on a per-issue basis.

Listening to Music with Pandora Radio

The iPod app isn't the only way to listen to music on your iPad. In addition to the many streaming Internet radio station apps, there is Pandora, which enables you make your own radio station based on a song or artist.

1. When you first run Pandora, you can choose to use your existing account or create a new one. Choose which, and then you will be prompted for some information.

2. When you are past the sign in/sign up stage, you see your stations to the left. To create a new station, tap in the field at the upper-left corner. Type in a name.

3. Pandora creates the new station and starts playing a song. If you like the song and think it represents what you want for this station, tap the Thumbs Up button.

4. If you think this isn't a song that should be played on this station, tap the Thumbs Down button.

5. Tap the Skip button if you think the song fits, but just don't want to hear it at the moment.

Pandora Everywhere

The stations you create on the iPad also show up in your Pandora account wherever you log on. You can use Pandora on your computer by just going to http://www.pandora.com/ and logging in. You can also use Pandora on many mobile phones. There are even television sets and car radios that play your Pandora radio stations.

Using Game Center

Apple has created a single unified system for high scores, achievements, and multiplayer gameplay. A large portion of the best games in the App Store have adopted this system, called Game Center.

Your game center account is the same one you use to purchase apps in the App Store. After you use the Game Center app to log in, you won't have to log in directly in any of the games. It all works seamlessly.

1. Tap the Game Center app to launch it. The app comes with your iPad.

2. Enter your ID and password and Sign In.

3. You'll see the number of games you have that connect to Game Center, plus the number of achievements you have accomplished in the game.

4. Tap Friends to see a list of people you have connected with in Game Center. You can challenge them to play a game.

5. Tap Games to see your scores and achievements for each game.

6. In the list of games, you can see your high scores. Tap a game to get more details.

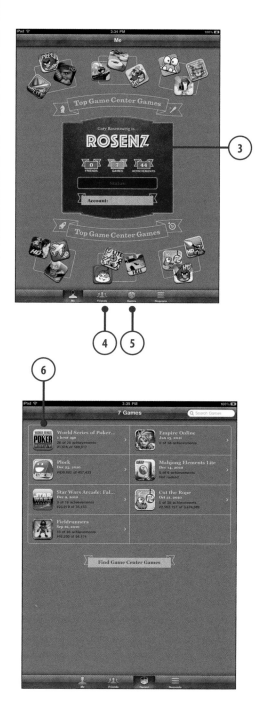

7. You can view a list of the world's best scores and see how you compare. Tap Achievements to see which ones you have and which you are missing.

You can often also see high scores and achievements inside the games themselves, even though they are stored in the Game Center system. You can challenge friends to games or to beat your scores from inside some games.

Playing iPad Games

Even if you purchased your iPad to stay connected, get work done, or watch videos, you might want to check out the rich and wonderful world of games.

With the touch screen and accelerometer control, the iPhone and iPod Touch turned out to be fertile ground for game developers. Add to that the large screen and fast processor of the iPad and you have a powerful and unique gaming device.

Let's take a look at some of the best games for the iPad.

Air Hockey

At first glance, this game looks simple. You control a paddle by moving your finger across the screen. You can play against a computer opponent that is actually quite challenging.

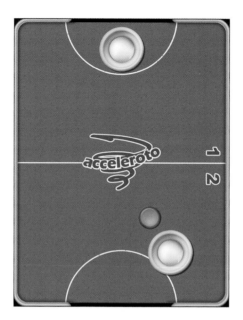

What's special is the ability to play against a second player at the other end of your iPad. Just set it down on a table and play head-to-head. This is made possible by the multitouch screen. The iPad needs to keep track of two fingers on the iPad. And it does it very smoothly.

Highborn

Do you like strategy and adventure? Highborn is a turn-based strategy game that takes you through a story of fantasy and magic. You deploy various units through short scenarios to conquer the board or achieve goals.

The thing that sets Highborn apart from other turn-based strategy games is a deep sense of humor. It helps you through the unavoidable tutorial and even makes you read all of the unit descriptions.

Harbor Master

One of the new game genres that appeared on the iPhone was the draw-to-direct type of game. It first appeared with a game called Flight Control, which is also available on the iPad.

Harbor Master takes the genre a little further. The idea is you direct ships into docks by drawing with your finger. Simply draw a line from the ship to the dock and the ship follows the path.

The game gets harder as you go along, with more and more ships unloading cargo and then sailing away. You have to make sure the ships find a dock and that they never collide.

Angry Birds

Many people purchase games to play on an iPad. But some people buy an iPad to play a game. When that is the case, the game responsible is usually Angry Birds. It is a physics-based game that uses a cannon, or similar devices, to shoot projectiles at a structure.

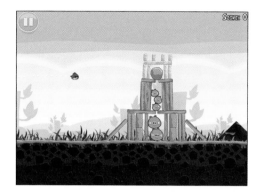

In this game, you shoot birds at a structure using a slingshot. Your goal is to destroy the pigs living in the building. Sounds a bit strange, but behind the premise is a good physics simulation that presents challenges with every level.

Galcon Fusion

Galcon was a huge hit on the iPhone, and all the time you couldn't help but wonder how much better it would be on a larger touch screen. Now we know, because we have Galcon Fusion for the iPad.

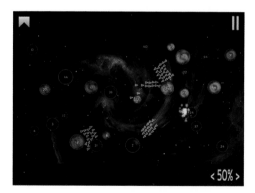

In this game, you conquer a small cluster of planets using ships. The game looks like a strategy game, and you must use strategy to win. But it plays like an arcade game because all you do is tap and drag to send ships from one planet to another.

Plants vs. Zombies

Zombies are attacking your house, and you need to defend it. So what do you use? Strange mutant fighting plants, of course.

It sounds weird, and it is. But as a fun strategy game, it works. It plays like a tower-defense style game but with fun elements that you find in those $20 PC game downloads.

Monkey Island 2 Special Edition

If you played this game back when it was first a hit on the PC, then you'll be excited to know that it has been re-imagined for the iPad. It is the same adventure, but with beautiful graphics and sound.

If you have never heard of Monkey Island, then you really shouldn't wait any longer. This game probably represents the pinnacle of computer adventure games and can give you hours of head-scratching and gut-busting fun.

Scrabble

My favorite game on the iPhone was Scrabble. The same game comes to the iPad but with some special new features. Not only can you play against a tough computer opponent, a friend on Facebook, or your local network, but you can also play against a friend in the same room, using your iPhones.

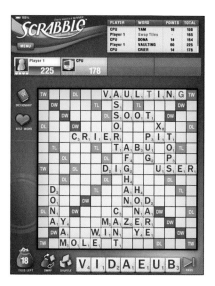

You just both download the Tile Rack app for the iPhone and then use the iPad as the main game board; your tiles appear only on your iPhones.

Field Runners

A major genre of touch device gaming is tower defense. In these games, you build walls and armaments to defend against a never-ending onslaught of enemy troops. Probably the best in this group is Field Runners.

The enemies come out of specific spots at the sides of the board and try to move across it. You have to gun them down before they reach the other side. But you are on a budget. So choose your weapons and place them carefully.

Real Racing 2 HD

A much more advanced use of accelerometers is when you use them to steer a car while racing. There are many racing games for the iPhone, and some have already made their way over to the iPad.

Real Racing HD is one that has excellent graphics and game play. It also has lots of options, including a career mode, car choices, and so on. It is close to some console racing games in features and graphics.

Gold Strike

I'll go ahead and mention one of my own games here. Gold Strike was first a web-based game, then a PC game, and then an iPhone game. Once you try it, you'll see that it was really an iPad game all along, just waiting for the iPad to come along.

You tap groups of blocks to remove them before the mine fills up. Gold blocks give you points, and the larger the group, the more points you get. The iPad version also includes some game variations for extended play.

Extend your iPad with docks, cases, connectors, and keyboards.

In this chapter, we use some optional accessories like cases, docks, keyboards, and adapters.

→ Printing from Your iPad
→ iPad Smart Cover
→ Apple iPad 2 Dock
→ Apple Video Output Adapters
→ Apple Wireless Keyboard
→ Apple iPad Keyboard Dock
→ Power/Dock Accessories
→ Protecting Your iPad
→ Apple iPad Camera Connection Kit

iPad Accessories

Many accessories available for your iPad perform a variety of tasks, protect it, or just make it look pretty.

You might already have some things that work with your iPad—Bluetooth headsets and keyboards, for instance. Let's look at a variety of accessories to see how to use them.

Printing from Your iPad

Some time after the release of the first iPad, Apple added wireless printing to the iOS operating system. They call it AirPrint. You can print a web page or document directly from your iPad over your wireless network.

The one catch? It works only with a select few printers that have recently been released by HP. You can find an updated list of AirPrint printers at http://support.apple.com/kb/ht4356.

Assuming you have one of these printers and have set it up on your local network, here's how you print, using the Pages app as an example.

1. In Pages, with the document you want to print open, tap the Tools button.

2. Tap Print.

3. If you have never used this particular printer before, you'll need to add it to the iPad's list of printers. Tap Select Printer.

4. If the printer is on and has been configured to your network, it should appear in a list. Tap it to add it.

5. The printer will now appear in the list. If you have more than one printer selected, you may need to select which one you want to use.

6. Tap Range to specify a range of pages to print, or leave it at All Pages.

7. Tap here to set the number of copies to print, or leave at 1 Copy.

8. Tap the Print button to send to the printer.

At this point, your iPad will launch a special Printer Center app. You may not notice it unless you quickly double-press the Home button to bring up the Recents List. You will then see this Print Center app running.

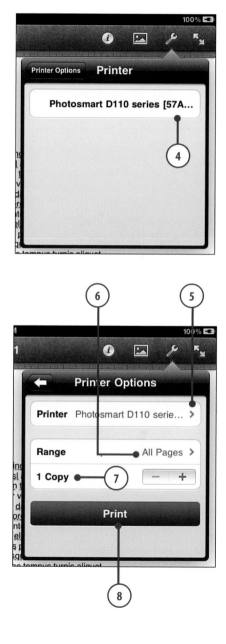

9. Double-press the Home button to bring up the Recents List.

10. Tap the Print Center icon to bring up a status menu.

11. You can see the status of the printing process and other information.

12. Tap Cancel Printing to stop printing.

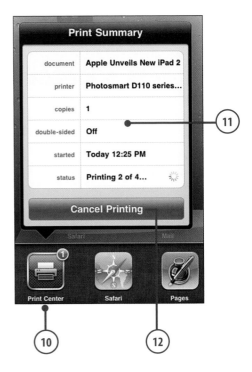

Different for Other Apps

How you initiate printing differs from app to app. Using Safari, for example, you go to the same button at the top of the screen that you use for bookmarking a page. You see Print as one of the options. In the Photos app it is the same button that enables you to email a photo, among other things.

Bypassing Apple's AirPrint

Although only a few Wi-Fi printers support AirPrint, there is a way to cheat. Some enterprising third-party developers have come up with software for Macs that sets up a printer connected to the Mac as an AirPrint printer. You aren't really printing directly to a printer—you are going through the Mac. Still, it may be a good option for some. Search on the Web for the Macintosh software Printopia , FingerPrint, or AirPrint Activator.

iPad Smart Cover

A cover is just a cover, right? But Apple didn't make "just a cover" for the iPad 2. They made a "smart cover." By using magnets, this cover sticks to the front of the iPad 2 without hiding the rest of the iPad's design. And it is highly functional, acting as a stand as well.

1. The cover will align to the front of you iPad using magnets and protect the screen.

2. Unfold the cover and two things will happen: the lining will clean your screen slightly, and the iPad will automatically wake up from sleep.

3. Fold the cover all the way back to form a triangle and elevate one side of the iPad for typing.

4. Flip the iPad over and it will lean against the triangle-configured cover to stand the iPad up for watching video or using FaceTime.

(Courtesy of Apple Inc.)

It Comes in Colors

You can get the Smart Cover in five colors in polyurethane and five colors in leather. Plus, with the magnets built into the iPad there are sure to be third-party case makers that come out with even more styles in the future.

(Courtesy of Apple Inc.)

(Courtesy of Apple Inc.)

Apple iPad 2 Dock

Although the iPad comes with a dock cable and charger, you might want to dock it in an upright position, rather than having it flat on a table. The iPad 2 Dock from Apple enables you to stand the iPad up vertically while it's either plugged in to a power outlet or docked with your computer. You can also use the iPad in this position and even pipe the audio into external speakers through the dock.

(Courtesy of Apple Inc.)

1. Plug the dock cable that came with your iPad into the back of the iPad Dock.

2. Plug the other end of the dock cable into the USB port of your computer.

3. Plug in the input cable from a set of computer speakers into the audio jack in the back of the iPad Dock.

4. Slip your iPad into the iPad Dock. A connection should establish between your computer and the iPad, just as if you used the cable by itself.

5. Run any audio-producing app, such as iPod. Music should now go through your external speakers, rather than just the built-on speakers of the iPad.

Power Dock

You can also connect the dock cable to the power supply that came with your iPad. Then the iPad Dock acts as a power station. You can also use the iPad while charging, or you can put it in picture frame mode. Or it can run some nice speakers and act as a music system.

Not All Power Is the Same

Your iPad requires extra power to charge properly. With the power supply that came with your iPad, it should charge fully after about 4 hours. But with an iPhone power supply, or while hooked up to a full-power USB port on a computer, it takes twice that amount of time. Some low-power USB ports on computers won't charge the iPad at all.

Apple Video Output Adapters

Apple sells several dock adapters that send video from the dock to a monitor, television, or projector. These are great for making presentations with your iPad 2 or watching video on a larger screen.

Dock to VGA Adapter

The Apple iPad Dock to VGA Adapter attaches on one end to the dock port on the bottom of your iPad. The other end is a VGA port you attach to a VGA cable that can be attached to a monitor or projector.

Whereas the original iPad could show only movies, presentations, and slideshows, the iPad 2 can use this adapter to show almost anything that is on the screen.

1. Connect the Apple iPad Dock to VGA Adapter to the dock port on your iPad.

2. Connect the other end of the adapter to a standard VGA cable.

(Courtesy of Apple Inc.)

Use the Dock
You can also connect the Apple iPad Dock to VGA Adapter to the Apple iPad Dock if you plan to use it this way often.

3. Connect the other end of the VGA cable to a monitor or projector that accepts a VGA connection.

4. Use an audio mini jack to connect the headphone port of the iPad to the line in on the projector. The exact type of cable you need depends on what audio input the project takes.

5. Run the Videos app on your iPad.

6. Tap the Play button just as you normally would to play back the video on the iPad. The video should start playing on the projector, while you see a frozen frame on your iPad.

Other Cable Options

Apple also makes an Apple Component AV Cable that works basically the same way but will output to RGB and left/right audio for high-definition televisions. There is also an Apple Composite AV Cable that uses a single connector for video for older standard definition televisions. Both cables will output video from some apps, but will not mirror the screen.

Digital AV Adapters

New for the iPad 2 is the Digital AV Adapter. This is an HDMI connector that enables you to connect directly to televisions and newer projectors that have an HDMI port. In addition, you can connect HDMI and another dock cable at the same time, allowing you to keep your iPad charged.

1. Connect the Apple Digital AV Adapter to the dock port on your iPad 2.

2. Connect the HDMI port on the adapter to an HDMI cable and connect that to a television or other device that supports HDMI.

3. Connect the dock port on the adapter to your iPad 2 charger or computer by using the dock cable that came with your iPad 2. This is optional, but it keeps your iPad from running out of power while presenting.

(Courtesy of Apple Inc.)

4. Use your iPad as you normally would, and most things will display on the television as well as on the iPad's screen. However, start watching a video, and the video itself will be presented without additional screen elements.

The video coming from the iPad is compatible with both 720p and 1080p HD televisions and video devices. It also includes audio over the HDMI cable. Many televisions support only 1080i, not 1080p. In that case, the video may be shown in 720p instead.

Apple Wireless Keyboard

If you have a lot of typing to do, and are sitting at a desk anyway, you can use Apple's Bluetooth keyboard with your iPad. This is the same wireless keyboard that you would use with a Mac.

1. To connect to the Apple Wireless Keyboard, make sure that you have good batteries in it.

(Courtesy of Apple Inc.)

Choosing the Right Wireless Keyboard

If you have an older Apple Wireless Keyboard, it might not work with your iPad. The Apple Store warns that only "newer" keyboards can successfully connect to the iPad. Reports from people with older wireless keyboards indicate that this is true. However, you don't need to stick with Apple's wireless keyboard. Most Bluetooth keyboards work fine with the iPad. Search your favorite online store for all kinds of compact wireless Bluetooth keyboards. Check reviews to see if anyone has mentioned trying the model with an iPad.

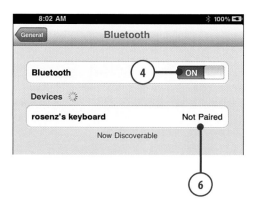

2. Go to the Settings app on your iPad and tap on the General settings on the left.

3. Tap Bluetooth to go to the Bluetooth settings.

4. Make sure Bluetooth is turned on. Switch it on if not.

5. Turn on your Apple Wireless Keyboard by pressing the button on its right side. You should see a small green light turn on at the upper-right corner of the main face of the keyboard.

6. After a second or two, the keyboard should appear on your iPad screen. Tap where you see Not Paired on the iPad screen.

7. Look for a 6-digit number in the message displayed. Type that on your keyboard. Then press the Return key.

8. After the connection is established, you should see Connected next to the name of your keyboard.

9. After you connect, the iPad automatically uses the physical keyboard by default, rather than brining up the on-screen keyboard. To use the on-screen keyboard again, you can either disconnect or power off your Apple Wireless Keyboard, or you can press the Eject button at the upper-right corner of the keyboard to switch to the on-screen keyboard at any time.

> **"rosenz's keyboard" would like to pair with your iPad.**
> Enter the passkey "877512" n
> "rosenz's keyboard", followed b / the
> return or enter key.
>
> **Cancel**

⑦

8:06 AM	✻ 100% 🔋
◀ General **Bluetooth**	
Bluetooth	**ON**
Devices	
rosenz's keyboard	Connected ❯
Now Discoverable	

⑧

>>> Go Further

SPECIAL KEYS

The Apple Wireless Keyboard was not made for the iPad—it existed first. But the iPad recognizes many special keys on it and uses those keys in various ways.

- Brightness (F1 and F2): Changes the brightness of the iPad screen
- Volume (F10, F11 and F12): Mutes, lowers, and raises the volume
- Eject (To the right of F12): Brings up or dismisses the on-screen keyboard
- Arrows: Navigates around in editable text
- Arrows+Shift: Selects editable text
- Command: Can be used with X, C, and V for cut, copy, and paste inside editable text
- Audio Playback Keys (F7, F7 and F9): Goes to previous track, play/pause, and next track

Apple iPad Keyboard Dock

Another way to use a keyboard is to get the special keyboard dock from Apple. This device combines an iPad Dock with a keyboard and connects the two via a physical dock rather than a wireless connection.

(Courtesy of Apple Inc.)

Vertical Screen Only

One problem with the Keyboard Dock is that by docking the iPad on it, you have to use the iPad in vertical screen orientation. So you can't type in horizontal screen orientation, which some people might prefer. (Some apps work only in horizontal mode.)

Besides not being wireless, this keyboard has many iPad-specific special keys:

- **Home button:** This is at the upper left and acts like the Home button on the iPad. It also wakes the iPad from the Lock screen.

- **Search button:** The second from the left, this button takes you to the Search screen.

- **Brightness:** Two buttons moved slightly over from their positions on the Bluetooth keyboard.

- **Picture Frame:** A special button that activates picture frame mode.

- **Keyboard:** A button that switches you to the on-screen keyboard.

- **Lock button:** This turns off the iPad, much like the wake/sleep button would.

There are also audio playback controls and volume controls in the same locations as on the wireless keyboard. Missing from the keyboard is an fn button used on a Mac to switch the top row of keys to F1–F12 keys.

Wireless Versus Dock

So which is better: the wireless keyboard or the docked keyboard? The wireless keyboard seems to have a distinct edge. You can use your iPad in horizontal or vertical mode. You can keep your iPad in its case. You can adjust the position of the iPad relative to the keyboard. And you can use a wireless keyboard with other devices, not just the iPad.

There's a third way you can use a keyboard with your iPad. You can connect low-power USB keyboards through the USB connector that comes with the iPad Camera Connection Kit.

Power/Dock Accessories

A power user of any gadget usually acquires additional power chargers and cables. For instance, you might want to charge your iPad at home and at work. Remembering to carry the adapter with you everywhere you go usually doesn't work out. Here is a list of items you might want to consider:

- **Apple iPad 10W USB power adapter**: A 10-watt adapter that charges the iPad at full speed, faster than a standard USB port. This adapter comes with a 6-foot-long cord, which makes it different than the one you get with your iPad. You get a dock cable along with it.

- **Apple dock connector to USB cable**: If you just want the dock cable to plug your iPad into a Mac or PC for syncing and slow charging. It is always good to have a spare one of these, as losing your one and only one means you can't charge or sync your iPad. But if you have a recent iPhone or iPod, you already have another dock cable. But the older dock cables might not work with the iPad.

(Courtesy of Apple Inc.)

(Courtesy of Griffin)

- **Car Charger**: If you want to charge your iPad in your car, get a car charger. You can find several: The Griffin PowerJolt Car Charger, the Kensington PowerBolt Micro Car Charger, and the Incase Car Charger. Incase also makes a "combo" charger that works from both AC power and cars.

- **Guitar Connection Cable**: You can use a guitar or other musical instrument with the GarageBand app and some third-party apps. You need hardware to connect the guitar to your iPad; the Griffin GuitarConnect Cable for iPhone, iPod, and iPad does the trick. There is also the Apogee JAM Guitar Input device, which advertises higher quality input.

Protecting Your iPad

Instead of the Smart Cover, or in addition to it, you may want to get a protective case for your iPad. The problem here is not finding one, but choosing from the hundreds of models already available.

An example is the Belkin Slim Folio Stand for iPad 2. It is similar to the folding case for the original iPad. It protects the sides and back from scratches, and the cover folds over to protect the screen.

Belkin Slim Folio Stand

If you want something inexpensive and simple, the Keen iPad Sleeve is basically just a neoprene envelope for your iPad 2. This kind of case makes it easy to use your iPad without anything in the way, and protects it when you move from place to place.

Keen iPad Sleeve

If you want something that stays on your iPad all the time, the iLuv Flex-Gel case is a good example of one that fits onto the back and protects the back and sides.

If you like that idea but don't want to cover up the Apple logo on the back, then look at the Scosche snapSheild P2. It is semi-clear plastic that tints the back of your iPad without completely obscuring it.

And finally, just to show you how functional cases can get, there is the Kensington KeyFolio, a case with a built-in Bluetooth keyboard. It basically turns your iPad into a laptop.

When looking for a case, there are many things to consider. Don't just look in a local

Kensington KeyFolio

iLuv Flex-Gel Case

Scosche snapShield P2

Apple Store—it stocks only a few cases. Look online to discover a wide variety. Pick one that fits your needs and style.

Many of the newer cases might also cover the iPad plus the Smart Cover. This solves the problem of which to get: get both!

Apple iPad Camera Connection Kit

The Apple iPad Camera Connection Kit has two parts, both of which connect to your iPad via the dock port. The first part is an SD card reader. You connect one end to the iPad dock port and you plug a standard SD card, the type most cameras use, into the other end. The second part has a USB connection on the second end. You can connect a digital camera to your iPad using it.

Here is how to import photos directly from your camera or SD card.

(Courtesy of Apple Inc.)

1. Connect either the camera connector or the SD card reader to your iPad's dock port.

2. Connect your camera using the USB cable that came with it, or slide the SD card into the card reader. If you are connecting a camera, you will most likely need to switch the camera on and into the same mode you use to transfer pictures to a computer.

3. After a slight delay, the Photos app should launch and images on the camera or card should appear on your iPad's screen. Tap the images you want to import.

4. Tap the Delete Selected button if you want to delete the images without ever importing them into your iPad.

5. Tap the Import button.

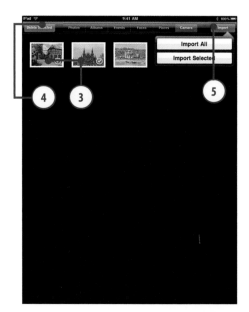

6. Tap Import All to import all photos. The images appear in a new album on your iPad.

7. Tap Import Selected to bring in only the selected photos.

8. After importing the photos, you will be given the change to delete them from the camera or card. Tap Delete to remove them.

9. Tap Keep to leave the images on the camera or card.

More Than Just Cameras!

The Connection Kit does a lot more than just let you use cameras and SD cards. You can also connect USB headsets with the camera connector and use them as headphones and/or a microphone. You can connect low-power USB keyboards as well. The SD card reader can be used to transfer video and images, so you can use it to play stored movies from SD cards.

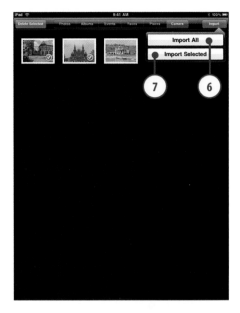

Index

Numbers

1Password app, 329

3G connections
Data Roaming, 45
setting up, 44-45

A

About section (Settings screen), 24-25

accessories
AirPrint, 354-356
Apple Component AV Cable, 360
Apple Composite AV Cable, 360
Apple Digital AV Adapter, 360-361
Apple iPad 2 Dock, 358
Apple iPad Camera Connection Kit,
358-369
Apple iPad Dock to VGA Adapter,
258-260, 359-360
Apple iPad Keyboard Dock, 364-365
Apple Wireless Keyboard, 361-363
iPad Smart Cover, 357
power chargers, 365-366
protective cases, 366-368

adapters
Apple Digital AV Adapter, 360-361
Apple iPad Dock to VGA Adapter,
258-260, 359-360

adding
contacts, 98-99
photos to video in iMovie, 177-179
sound to video in iMovie, 181
video titles in iMovie, 180-181

Air Hockey app, 344-345

AirPlay, 76
stream slideshows, 161

AirPrint, 354-356

albums
organizing photos into, 154
viewing, 62, 159-160

alert sounds, adjusting, 26-27

aligning text in documents, 196-197

Angry Birds app, 346-347

app screens, 10

App Store
finding apps, 286-287
purchasing apps, 278-280

Apple Component AV Cable, 360

Apple Composite AV Cable, 360

Apple Digital AV Adapter, 360-361

Apple Dock Connector to
USB Cable, 365

Apple iPad 10W USB Power
Adapter, 365

Apple iPad 2 Dock, 358

Apple iPad Camera
Connection Kit,
368-369

Apple iPad Dock to VGA
Adapter,
258-260, 359-360

Apple iPad Keyboard Dock,
364-365

Apple Wireless Keyboard,
361-363

appointments. *See* events

apps
1Password, 329
Bento, 298-301
deleting, 281
Dictionary.com, 311-312
Dragon Dictation app,
321-322
Epicurious, 327
Evernote, 329
Facebook, 329
finding, 286-287
Flipboard, 307-308
GarageBand, 334
GoodReader, 301
grouping, 50, 284-285
iPhone/iPod touch apps,
288-289
iTap VNC, 296-297
iTunes, arranging
with, 282
MindNode, 313-314
for newspapers, 306
NewsRack, 303-306
OmniGraffle, 309-311
purchasing, 278-280
quitting, 4, 286
rearranging, 281-283
recommending, 291-292
Redeem code, 279
in Settings list, 38
sharing, 292
SketchBook Pro, 329
Skype, 315-316
sorting, 283
StarWalk, 329
Stick It, 317-320

synchronization, 50
Things, 329
troubleshooting, 290
Twitter, 329
USA Today, 330
viewing running, 285-286
Voice Memos, 323-324
The Weather Channel
Max+, 330
Wolfram Alpha, 329
WritePad, 325-326
Zinio, 330

artwork, drawing, 329

audio. *See also* music
adding to video in
iMovie, 181
alert sounds, adjusting,
26-27
podcasts
downloading, 69-71
subscribing to, 71

automatic time settings, 34

average function
(spreadsheets), 221-224

averaging columns in
spreadsheets, 221-224

B

background images
inserting in
documents, 209
photos as, 158
sticky notes on, 317-320

battery, charging, 358,
365-366

Bento app, 298-301

Bluetooth address of iPad, 25

Bluetooth keyboards,
361-363

bookmarks
inserting in books, 91
setting in Maps app,
269-270
synchronization, 48-49

of web pages, 122-123
deleting, 123-124
saving to home screen,
125-126
syncing, 125

books
bookmarks, inserting, 91
ePub format, 82
highlights, inserting,
89-90
notes, inserting, 89-90
organizing, 92-93
purchasing, 82-84
reading, 85-87
customizing view, 87-88
with GoodReader
app, 301
on Kindle app, 94
on Nook app, 94

browsing
photos, 154-156
with Safari, 114-115

building
presentations, 244-245
slides, 246-249

bulleted lists, creating in
documents, 198-199

button lists, 14

buttons. *See* controls

buying. *See* purchasing

C

calculations in spread-
sheets, 225
updating, 233

Calendar
duplicate, 49
events, creating, 102-104
synchronization, 48-49
views, 105-108

Camera app
recording video, 168-169
taking photos, 149-151

camera connections, 368-369

Camera Roll, 154
  trimming video, 170
capacity of iPad,
  determining, 25
capitalizing letters, 15
capturing the screen, 163
car chargers, 366
cells in spreadsheets,
  formatting, 226-228
centering map on current
  location, 265
charging the battery, 358,
  365-366
charts, creating
  in documents, 207-208
  with OmniGraffle app,
    309-311
  in spreadsheets, 234-236
clip art, importing, 203
clipboard, copying
  photos to, 158
column layouts in
  documents, 200
columns in spreadsheets
  averaging, 221-224
  totaling, 220
.com button, 115
comic books, reading,
  339-340
Comics + app, 339-340
composing
  email messages, 140-141
  music with GarageBand
    app, 334-336
compressing video, 169
computer, synchronization
  with. See synchronization
  with iTunes
configuring email, 136-138,
  144-146
connections
  3G connections, setting
    up, 44-45

Wi-Fi network
  connections
    security, 43
    setting up, 42-43
contacts
  adding, 98-99
  assigning photos to, 157
  editing, 101
  searching, 100-101
  synchronization, 48-49, 99
controls. See also interface
  Home button, 4
  music playback, 62
  side switch, 6-7
  volume control, 6
    alert sounds, adjusting,
      26-27
  Wake/Sleep button, 5
copy protection for
  videos, 68
copying
  photos to clipboard, 158
  text, 17-18
  text styles, 195
  text/images from web
    pages, 131
covers
  iPad Smart Cover, 357
  protective cases, 366-368
current location, centering
  map on, 265
custom alert sounds, 27
customization
  alert sounds, adjusting,
    26-27
  date/time, setting, 33-34
  in iBooks, 87-88
  iPod settings, 37
  keyboard settings, 34-35
  parental restrictions,
    setting, 30-31
  password protection,
    setting, 28-30
  Safari settings, 36
  side switch, setting
    functionality, 32
  slideshow settings, 38

Video settings, 38
wallpaper, changing,
  22-24

D

Day view (Calendar), 105
Data Roaming with 3G
  connections, 45
databases, Bento app,
  298-301
date/time
  formatting in
    spreadsheets, 238
  setting, 33-34
deleting
  apps, 281
  bookmarks (Safari),
    123-124
  email messages, 142
  photos, 164-165
diagrams, creating with
  OmniGraffle app, 309-311
dictation apps, 321-322
Dictionary (iBooks), 89
Dictionary.com app, 311-312
Digital AV Adapter, 360-361
digital camera connections,
  368-369
directions (in Maps app),
  obtaining, 267-268
disabling
  MobileMe email
    account, 57
  viewing remote
    images, 146
docking
  the iPad, 358
  keyboards, 364-365
Document Setup options
  (Pages app), 209-210
documents. See also
  spreadsheets
  background images,
    inserting, 209

charts, creating, 207-208
column layouts, 200
creating, 190-191
Document Setup options, 209-210
horizontal view, 190
images
  inserting, 201-203
  moving, 203
line spacing, 200
lists, creating, 198-199
printing, 194
shapes
  inserting, 204
  styling, 205
synchronization, 51
tables
  creating, 205-207
  moving, 207
text
  aligning, 196-197
  copying styles, 195
  entering, 190-191
  styling, 192-194
transferring with iTunes, 210-212
double-tapping, 8
downloading podcasts, 69-71
dragging, 8
Dragon Dictation app, 321-322
draw-to-direct games, 346
drawing artwork, 329
DVDs, importing video from, 67

E

editing
  contacts, 101
  photos, 155
  playlists, 63
  text, 16-17
  video in iMovie, 171-174
  video transitions in iMovie, 175-177
email
  compressing video, 169

configuring, 136-138, 145-146
folders, creating, 140
messages
  composing, 140-141
  deleting, 142
  moving, 142
  reading, 139
  receiving, 144
  searching, 143
  signatures, creating, 141
multiple inboxes, 140
sending photos, 157
spam filtering, 142
email accounts
  MobileMe, disabling, 57
  synchronization, 48-49
email inbox, notes in, 111
emergency contact info on Lock and Home screens, 320
Epicurious app, 327
ePub format, 82
equations in spreadsheets, 225
events, creating in Calendar, 102-104
Evernote app, 329
exporting documents from Pages app, 212
external displays, Apple iPad Dock Connector to VBA Adapter, 258-260, 359-360

F

Facebook app, 329
FaceTime accounts
  creating, 181-183
  placing calls with, 183-184
  receiving calls with, 185-186
  troubleshooting, 186
fetch delivery (email), 144
Field Runners app, 349-350

file sharing, troubleshooting, 51
filenames for notes, 109
Find My iPad, 57
finding
  apps, 286-287
  locations, 264-265
  multiple locations, 266
flash when taking photos, 153
flicking, 9
Flipboard app, 307-308
folders
  for email, creating, 140
  grouping apps into, 284-285
footers
  in documents, 209
  in spreadsheets, formatting, 230
forgotten passcode, restoring, 30
formatting. See also styling
  cells in spreadsheets, 226-228
  date/time in spreadsheets, 238
  headers/footers in spreadsheets, 230
  notes, 111
  tables in spreadsheets, 229-230
  text in documents, 196-197
forms
  in Safari, filling in, 126-128
  in spreadsheets, creating, 231-233
formulas. See calculations

G

Galcon Fusion app, 347
Game Center app, 342-344
games
  Air Hockey app, 344-345
  Angry Birds app, 346-347

Field Runners app, 349-350

Galcon Fusion app, 347

Game Center app, 342-344

Gold Strike app, 350-351

Harbor Master app, 346

Highborn app, 345-346

Monkey Island 2 Special Edition app, 348

Plants vs. Zombies app, 348

Real Racing HD app, 350

Scrabble app, 349

GarageBand app, composing music with, 334-336

Genius playlists, 64

Gold Strike app, 350-351

GoodReader app, 301

Google Maps in Safari, 268

grouping
apps, 50, 284-285
slides, 255

GUI. *See* interface

guitar connection cables, 366

H

Handbrake, 67

handwriting recognition, 325-326

Harbor Master app, 346

HD (high definition) video, 68

HDMI adapters, 260, 360-361

headers
in documents, 209
in spreadsheets, formatting, 230

headsets, USB headset connections, 369

help. *See* troubleshooting

Highborn app, 345-346

highlights, inserting in books, 89-90

History button (Safari), 120-121

Home button, 4

Home screen, 10
saving bookmarks to, 125-126
sticky notes on, 317-320

Home Sharing, playing music/video, 77-78

home video, 67

horizontal view of documents, 190

I

iBooks
bookmarks, inserting, 91
highlights, inserting, 89-90
notes, inserting, 89-90
organizing books, 92-93
purchasing books from, 83-84
reading books, 85-87
customizing view, 87-88
troubleshooting, 89

icons for home screen bookmarks, 126

images. *See also* photos
background images, inserting in documents, 209
clip art, importing, 203
copying from web pages, 131
including in email messages, 141
inserting in documents, 201-203
moving in documents, 203
remote images, disabling viewing, 146
saving from web pages, 132
slideshow settings, customizing, 38
wallpaper, changing, 22-24

IMAP (Internet Message Access Protocol), 136

iMovie app
adding
photos to video, 177-179
sound to video, 181
video titles, 180-181
editing
video, 171-174
video transitions, 175-177
sharing video, 174

importing
clip art, 203
documents to Pages app, 210-211
video from DVDs, 67

inboxes (email), multiple, 140

inserting
background images in documents, 209
bookmarks in books, 91
highlights in books, 89-90
images in documents, 201-203
notes in books, 89-90
shapes in documents, 204

interface. *See also* controls; customization
button lists, 14
dragging, 8
flicking, 9
on-screen keyboard, 15-16
pinching, 8
screens. *See* screens
sliders, 13
switches, 13
tab bars, 14
tapping, 8
text
copying/pasting, 17-18
editing, 16-17
toolbars, 14

Internet connections
3G connections, setting up, 44-45

Wi-Fi network
connections
security, 43
setting up, 42-43
Internet Message Access
Protocol (IMAP), 136
iPad
customizing. *See*
customization
docking, 358
keyboards for, 191
locking, 28
orientation, 7
shaking, 7
shutting down, 5
starting, 5
synchronization. *See*
synchronization with
iTunes
iPad OS version number, 25
iPad Smart Cover, 357
iPad version of web
pages, 115
iPhone apps, 288-289
iPod settings, customizing, 37
iPod touch apps, 288-289
iTap VNC app, 296-297
iTunes
purchasing from, 65-67
rearranging apps in,
282-283
sharing accounts, 292
synchronization with,
46-47
apps, 50
*contacts/calendars/
bookmarks/email
accounts, 48-49*
documents, 51
music, 52-53
photos, 53-54
transferring documents
with, 210-212
iWork.com service,
transferring
documents, 212

J–K

keyboard settings,
customizing, 34-35
keyboard shortcuts
on Apple iPad Keyboard
Dock, 364
on Apple Wireless
Keyboard, 363
keyboards, 191, 361-363. *See
also* on-screen keyboard
Apple iPad Keyboard
Dock, 364-365
Numbers app
options, 217
USB keyboards, 365, 369
Keynote app. *See*
presentations
Kindle app, 94

L

letters, capitalizing, 15
line spacing in
documents, 200
links in web pages, 119
List view (Calendar), 108
listening to music, 340-341.
See also songs, playing
lists, creating in documents,
198-199
locations, finding, 264-266
lock screen, 9-10
sticky notes on, 317-320
locking iPad, 28

M

magazine apps, 330
Magic Move transition (in
presentations), 251-252
Mail. *See* email
Maps app, 263
bookmarks, setting,
269-270
centering on current
location, 265
directions, obtaining,
267-268
locations, finding,
264-265
multiple locations,
finding, 266
Satellite View, 271-272
Street View, 273-274
traffic reports, 275
meetings. *See* events
menus, 14
messages (email)
composing, 140-141
deleting, 142
moving, 142
reading, 139
receiving, 144
searching, 143
signatures, creating, 141
mind mapping, 313-314
microphones, 316
MindNode app, 313-314
MobileMe
calendar
synchronization, 49
email account,
disabling, 57
synchronization with,
55-57
model numbers, 25-26
Monkey Island 2 Special
Edition app, 348
Month view (Calendar), 107
movies, watching with Netflix
app, 337-338. *See also* video
moving. *See also* rearranging
email messages, 142
images in documents, 203
tables in documents, 207
MP4 format, 72
Multi-Pass, 68
multiple inboxes (email), 140
multiple locations,
finding, 266

multiple tables in spreadsheets, 236-237, 240-241

multiple web pages, opening, 129-130

music. *See also* audio; songs
adding to video in iMovie, 181
via AirPlay, playing, 76
composing with GarageBand app, 334-336
via Home Sharing, playing, 77-78
listening to, 340-341
playlists
building, 63-64
editing, 63
Genius playlists, 64
purchasing from iTunes, 65-67
synchronization, 52-53

mute switch, 6-7
setting, 32

N

Netflix app, 72, 337-338

network connections
3G connections, setting up, 44-45
Wi-Fi network connections
security, 43
setting up, 42-43

newspapers, apps for, 306-308, 330

NewsRack app, 303-306

Nook app, 94

notes
creating, 109-110
in email inbox, 111
filenames for, 109
formatting, lack of, 111
handwriting, 325-326
inserting in books, 89-90

on Home/Lock screen, 317
recording, 323-324

numbered lists, creating in documents, 198-199

numbers and punctuation, typing, 15

Numbers app, keyboard options, 217. *See also* spreadsheets

O

object transitions (in presentations), 253-254

OmniGraffle app, 309-311

on-screen keyboard, 15-16
keyboard settings, customizing, 34-35

On/Off button. *See* Wake/Sleep button

opening multiple web pages, 129-130

organizing
apps
on iPad, 281-282
in iTunes, 282-283
books, 92-93
photos into albums, 154, 159-160
slides, 255-256

orientation
of iPad, 7
of video, changing, 73

orientation lock, 6-7
setting, 32

original photos, 157

P

Pages app. *See also* documents
Document Setup options, 209-210
transferring documents with iTunes, 210-212
Undo button, 192

Pandora app, 340-341

paper size, changing for documents, 209

parental restrictions, setting, 30-31

parentheses in spreadsheet calculations, 225

passcode, restoring, 30

password protection, setting, 28-30

passwords, storing, 329

pasting text, 17-18

pausing songs, 62

PDF files, reading with GoodReader app, 301

Penultimate, 326

phone calls, video
creating FaceTime accounts, 181-183
placing, 183-184
receiving, 185-186

Photo Booth app, taking photos, 152-153

photos. *See also* images
adding to video in iMovie, 177-179
browsing, 154-156
deleting, 164-165
editing, 155
organizing into albums, 154, 159-160
originals, 157
in Picture Frame, 161-162
slideshows, creating, 160-161
synchronization, 53-54
taking
with Camera app, 149-151
with Photo Booth app, 152-153
usage examples, 157-158
zooming, 156

physics games, 346-347

Picture Frame, viewing photos in, 161-162

pinching, 8

placing video phone calls, 183-184

Plants vs. Zombies app, 348

playing
music/video
via AirPlay, 76
via Home Sharing, 77-78
presentations, 257
with VGA Adapter, 258-260
songs, 60-62
video, 72-73
YouTube video, 74-75

playlists. *See also* music
building, 63-64
editing, 63
Genius playlists, 64

podcasts
downloading, 69-71
subscribing to, 71

POP (Post Office Protocol), 136

power supplies, 365-366
battery charging with, 358

presentations
building, 244-245
playing, 257
with VGA Adapter, 258-260
slides
building, 246-249
organizing, 255-256
transitions, 250-254
themes, 246

previewing video transitions, 177

printing
with AirPrint, 354-356
documents, 194
web pages, 122

protective cases, 366-368

punctuation, typing, 15

purchasing
apps, 278-280
books, 83-84
from iTunes, 65-67
video, 68

push delivery (email), 144

Q–R

quitting apps, 4, 286

racing games, 350

radio stations. *See* Pandora app

reading
books, 85-87
customizing view, 87-88
with GoodReader app, 301
on Kindle app, 94
on Nook app, 94
comic books, 339-340
email messages, 139

Real Racing HD app, 350

rearranging apps
on iPad, 281-282
in iTunes, 282-283

receiving
email messages, 144
video phone calls, 185-186

recipes, Epicurious app, 327

recommending apps, 291-292

recording
notes, 323-324
video, 168-169

remote images, disabling viewing, 146

rented video, 68

resolution of photos, 151

restoring passcode, 30

restrictions. *See* parental restrictions

routes, mapping, 267-268

RSS feeds, 303-306

running apps, viewing, 285-286

S

Safari
bookmarking web pages, 122-123
browsing with, 114-115
copying text/images from web pages, 131
customizing settings, 36
deleting bookmarks, 123-124
filling in web forms, 126-128
Google Maps in, 268
links in, 119
opening multiple web pages, 129-130
printing web pages, 122
saving bookmarks to home screen, 125-126
saving images from web pages, 132
searching with, 115-117
syncing bookmarks, 125
viewing web pages, 117-119
previously visited pages, 120-121

Satellite View (Maps app), 271-272

Saved Photos, 163
deleting photos, 164-165

saving
bookmarks (Safari) to home screen, 125-126
images from web pages, 132

Scrabble app, 349

screen captures, 163

screens
app screens, 10
Home screen, 10
lock screen, 9-10
Search screen, 11

Settings screen, 12
About section, 24-25
apps in, 38

SD (standard definition) video, 68

SD card connections, 368-369

Search (iBooks), 89

Search screen, 11

searching
contacts, 100-101
email messages, 143
for places, 266
with Safari, 115-117

season passes for TV shows, 68

security
password protection, setting, 28, 30
Wi-Fi network connections, 43

selecting tables in spreadsheets, 237

serial number of iPad, 25

Settings screen, 12
About section, 24-25
apps in, 38

shaking iPad, 7

shapes
inserting in documents, 204
styling in documents, 205

sharing
apps, 292
files, troubleshooting, 51
video, 174

sheets in spreadsheets, 216

shutting down iPad, 5

side switch, 6-7
setting functionality, 32

signatures for email messages, creating, 141

SketchBook Pro app, 329

Skype app, 315-316

sleep mode, 5

sliders, 13

slides
building, 246-249
organizing, 255-256
transitions, 250-254
Magic Move transition, 251-252
object transitions, 253-254
viewing, 246

slideshows
customizing settings, 38
of photos, creating, 160-161
streaming with AirPlay, 161
viewing in Picture Frame, 161-162

smart covers, 357

songs. *See also* audio; music
pausing, 62
playing, 60-62

sorting apps, 283

sound. *See* audio

spam filters, 142

special keys
on Apple iPad Keyboard Dock, 364
on Apple Wireless Keyboard, 363

spreadsheets. *See also* documents
calculations in, 225
updating, 233
cells, formatting, 226-228
charts, creating, 234, 236
columns
averaging, 221-224
totaling, 220
creating, 216-219
date/time formatting, 238
forms, creating, 231-233
headers/footers, formatting, 230
tables
formatting, 229-230
multiple tables in, 236-237, 240-241
selecting, 237

starting iPad, 5

StarWalk app, 329

Stick It app, 317-320

sticky notes on Lock and Home screens, 317-320

storage space for video, 68

storing passwords, 329

strategy games, 345-348

Street View (Maps app), 273-274

styling
shapes in documents, 205
text in documents, 192-194
copying styles, 195

subscribing to podcasts, 71

sum function (spreadsheets), 220

switches, 13

synchronization
of bookmarks (Safari), 125
of contacts, 99
with iTunes, 46-47
apps, 50
contacts/calendars/bookmarks/email accounts, 48-49
documents, 51
music, 52-53
photos, 53-54
with MobileMe, 55-57

T

tab bars, 14

tables
creating in documents, 205-207
moving in documents, 207
in spreadsheets, 216
formatting, 229-230
multiple tables, 236-237, 240-241
selecting, 237

tabs in documents, 197

taking photos
  with Camera app, 149-151
  with Photo Booth app,
    152-153
tapping, 8
text
  copying from web
    pages, 131
  copying/pasting, 17-18
  in documents
    aligning, 196-197
    column layouts, 200
    copying styles, 195
    entering, 190-191
    line spacing, 200
    lists, creating, 198-199
    styling, 192, 194
  editing, 16-17
  typing, 15-16
themes in presentations, 246
thesaurus apps, 311-312
Things app, 329
thumbnail images, assigning
  to contacts, 157
time-delayed rentals
  (video), 68
time/date
  formatting in
    spreadsheets, 238
  setting, 33-34
titles, adding to video in
  iMovie, 180-181
to-do lists, creating, 109-110
toolbars, 14
totaling columns in
  spreadsheets, 220
tower defense games,
  349-350
traffic reports, 275
transferring documents with
  iTunes, 210-212
transitions
  in movies, editing in
    iMovie, 175-177

  in presentations, 250-254
  *Magic Move transition,
    251-252*
  *object transitions,
    253-254*
trimming video, 170
troubleshooting
  apps, 290
  calculations in
    spreadsheets, 233
  calendar
    synchronization, 49
  FaceTime, 186
  file sharing, 51
  forgotten passcode, 30
  Home Sharing, 78
  iBooks, 89
  notes in email inbox, 111
  viewing presentations
    with VGA Adapter, 260
  VNC connections, 297
turn-based strategy games,
  345-346
TV hookups with Apple iPad
  Dock Connector to VGA
  Adapter, 258-260
TV shows
  Multi-Pass, 68
  season passes, 68
  watching with Netflix app,
    337-338
Twitter app, 329
typing
  capital letters, 15
  with on-screen
    keyboard, 15
  text, 15-16
  URLs, 115

U

UI. *See* interface
Undo button (Pages app), 192
updating calculations in
  spreadsheets, 233
URL (Universal Resource
  Locator), 115

USA Today app, 330
USB headset connections, 369
USB keyboards, 365, 369
user interface. *See* interface

V

version number of
  iPad OS, 25
VGA adapters, 258-260,
  359-360
video
  alternatives to Apple, 72
  compressing, 169
  editing in iMovie, 171-174
  emailing, 169
  HD versus SD, 68
  home video, 67
  importing from DVDs, 67
  MP4 format, 72
  orientation, changing, 73
  photos, adding in iMovie,
    177-179
  playing, 72-73
    via AirPlay, 76
    *via Home Sharing,
      77-78*
    YouTube video, 74-75
  podcasts
    downloading, 69-71
    subscribing to, 71
  purchasing, 68
  recording, 168-169
  sharing, 174
  sound, adding in
    iMovie, 181
  space constraints, 68
  titles, adding in iMovie,
    180-181
  transitions, editing in
    iMovie, 175-177
  trimming, 170
video phone calls
  FaceTime accounts,
    creating, 181-183
  placing, 183-184
  receiving, 185-186
Video settings, customizing, 38

viewing. *See also* playing
albums, 62, 159-160
documents, horizontal
view, 190
maps
Satellite View, 271-272
Street View, 273-274
movies with Netflix app,
337-338
photos, 154-156
in Picture Frame,
161-162
as slideshow, 160-161
remote images,
disabling, 146
running apps, 285-286
slides, 246
web pages, 117-119
previously visited pages,
120-121
views in Calendar, 105-108
VNC (Virtual Network
Computing), 296-297
Voice Memos app, 323-324
VOIP (voice over IP) apps,
315-316
volume control, 6
alert sounds, adjusting,
26-27

W

Wake/Sleep button, 5
wallpaper, changing, 22-24
watching. *See* viewing
The Weather Channel Max+
app, 330
web pages
bookmarking, 122-123
deleting bookmarks,
123-124
saving bookmarks to
home screen, 125-126
syncing bookmarks, 125
browsing, 114-115
copying text/images, 131
filling in forms, 126-128
iPad versions, 115
links in, 119
opening multiple,
129-130
printing, 122
saving images, 132
searching for, 115-117
viewing, 117-119
previously visited pages,
120-121

Week view (Calendar), 106
Wi-Fi address of iPad, 25
Wi-Fi network connections
security, 43
setting up, 42-43
wireless keyboards, 361-363
Wolfram Alpha app, 329
word processing. *See*
documents
WritePad app, 325-326
writing email messages,
140-141

X–Z

YouTube video, playing,
74-75

Zinio app, 330
zooming photos, 156